PICTURE HISTORY OF
THE FRENCH LINE

PICTURE HISTORY OF
THE FRENCH LINE

William H. Miller, Jr.

DOVER PUBLICATIONS, INC.

for Tom Cassidy

dear friend, leader, French Line traveler

ACKNOWLEDGMENTS

Many hands have helped to assemble this pictorial parade. The author wishes to express his very special appreciation to three of the world's great ocean-liner collectors: Frank O. Braynard, Richard C. Faber, and Everett Viez, who have, as always, shown extraordinary kindness, generosity, and support.

Other much-appreciated photographic materials and resources have come from Ernest Arroyo, Philippe Brebant, Michael Cassar, Luis Miguel Correia, Frank Cronican, Alex Duncan, Tom Greene, Frank Heine, Eric Johnson, Robert Lenzer, Fred Rodriguez, Robert Russell, the late Victor Scrivens, and Joe Wilhelm. Companies and organizations that have assisted include Chantiers de l'Atlantique, Costa Line, Flying Camera, Inc., the French Line, Hapag-Lloyd Shipyards, Messageries Maritimes, Moran Towing & Transportation Company, the Port Authority of New York and New Jersey, Schiffsfotos Jansen, Steamship Historical Society of America, and Todd Shipyards, Inc.

And, of course, my warmest thanks to my family, to Abe Michaelson, and to the splendid staff at Dover Publications.

Published in Canada by General Publishing Company, Ltd., 30 Lesmill Road, Don Mills, Toronto, Ontario.
Published in the United Kingdom by Constable and Company, Ltd., 3 The Lanchesters, 162–164 Fulham Palace Road, London W6 9ER.

Library of Congress Cataloging-in-Publication Data

Miller, William H., 1948–
    Picture history of the French Line / William H. Miller.
       p. cm.
    Includes bibliographical references and index.
    ISBN 0-486-29443-9 (pbk.)
    1. Compagnie générale transatlantique—History—Pictorial works.
2. Steamboat lines—France—History—Pictorial works.   3. Ocean liners—France—History—Pictorial works I. Title.
HE945.C56M55 1997
387.5'06'541—dc21   97-5791
                                                       CIP

Bibliographical Note

Picture History of the French Line is a new work, first published by Dover Publications, Inc., in 1997.

Manufactured in the United States of America
Dover Publications, Inc.
31 East 2nd Street
Mineola, N.Y. 11501

CONTENTS

CREDITS

FOREWORD

In the sixties and seventies, when most transatlantic steamship lines abandoned their passenger services, it was widely thought that almost everything of interest to collectors had vanished. Some items went into cellars or the storerooms of museums, universities, and libraries. Others (like the big Cunard model collection from the firm's lower Broadway offices in New York) were scattered across North America to several museums. Worst of all, some collections went into incinerators and dumpsters. Of course, there were the memorabilia dealers, merchants of the past, who bought everything from champagne glasses to bedspreads to cocktail-lounge swizzle sticks as some of those grand liners were just about ready to go off to the scrappers. In the case of the legendary French Line, the Compagnie Générale Transatlantique, it was often reported that most of its archive was gone as well—variously discarded, sold at special auctions, stolen, a victim of World War II. But as I discovered during a visit to Le Havre one summer afternoon in 1994, this was not so. That visit inspired this book.

Le Havre might still be France's busiest seaport, but as with so many other seaports—Southampton, Liverpool, London, Lisbon, Genoa—today it is hard to tell. Great stretches of dockland, now lifeless and empty, once handled vast amounts of cargo: incoming spices from East Africa and India, tea and mass produce from the Far East, coffee from Brazil, and bananas from the Caribbean; outgoing wines, machinery, manufactured goods, railroad cars, Citroëns, and Renaults. The numerous cranes that once handled these goods are now grouped in rigid formation. Sheds bear the markings of long-gone firms: Chargeurs Réunis, the United States Lines, Black Diamond Line, the East Asiatic Company. Even the three freighters at dock on that summer afternoon were idle, awaiting sale to other owners. Cargoes are now handled by a few massive, highly efficient containerships that arrive less often and are handled in a separate corner of the port.

The outer pier head at Le Havre was equally desolate. It had been used by those long-vanished Atlantic liners: the *Liberté*, the *Ile de France*, the last *France*, the *United States*, the "second" *Mauretania*, and the "old" *Nieuw Amsterdam*. Little but the memory of those grand and famous ships remains. The terminal buildings and the sheds are locked tight, melancholy in their desuetude. The adjacent railway tracks, which handled the "boat trains" to and from Paris and which transported such celebrities as the Duke and Duchess of Windsor, Dietrich, and Garbo, are now rusted and weed infested. The old Gare Maritime, with its rooftop veranda, loading doors, railway entrances, and labyrinth of waiting rooms, offices, and storerooms, is equally sad—at least on the outside. It was home to the great French Line, the Compagnie Générale Transatlantique, or "Transat," as the French still call it. (It was "the French Line" to the Americans and the British.) The *France* made her last crossing from here in the late summer of 1974. Her urgently needed government operating subsidies were siphoned off to a newer symbol of intercontinental traveling prestige, the supersonic Concorde.

The CGT name still appears on the terminal's facade, but it is an otherwise somber, almost forbidding structure. Built in the late forties,

it replaced the earlier dock buildings and terminals that had been devastated by wartime bombings. But these ghostly French Line offices and storerooms, well hidden behind rather uninviting stairways and darkened hallways, boast a treasury of ocean-liner memorabilia, the past come to life.

"We have a mile of documents," noted Jean-Paul Herbert, the chief CGT archivist. "We have voyage reports back to the 1860s, captains' logs, menus, and passenger lists. We have most of the original construction plans and the contracts to build the ships. We also have a tremendous photo file on all CGT ships, especially the liners."

Transferred from the old corporate headquarters in Paris, all of this is now stored in the former passenger terminal at Le Havre—safe, secure, and systematically catalogued. But while one large area was devoted to printed items (including many evocative and now very pricey posters from the twenties and thirties), other areas held equally valuable pieces. One contained only furniture: wooden deck chairs with monogrammed cushions from the *Ile de France* (1927), tubular steel chairs from the *Champlain* (1932), desks from the *Normandie* (1935), and, perhaps most impressive of all, an entire suite of elaborate furniture, carved panels, gilded clocks, and marble busts from the four-funnel *France* of 1912. "We found the gold-trimmed, ornately designed panels in an abattoir," noted Mr. Herbert, "and then discovered other items in some of the oddest places—a butcher's shop, a bakery, attics. We also have a large closet full of uniforms from all ranks and departments, and all complete with brass buttons."

Still another large area was lined with great cabinets and cupboards that contained a pirate's ransom in glassware, crystal (including row upon row of crested Lalique), cutlery, and orderly formations of silver vases, teapots, and candelabra arranged like soldiers in a parade. I felt my pulse quicken as I touched a weighty carving knife or a crested salver from the magnificent *Normandie*. Against another wall there were rows of gold-framed paintings. In still another room, there were model ships of every size and caliber, including the massive builder's model of the *France* of 1961. But most spectacular was the 12-foot-long re-creation of the 1,028-foot-long *Normandie*. It had recently been restored by a team of ten model makers.

"A small maritime museum will open in Le Havre this fall [1994]," added Mr. Herbert. "But eventually we'll have a larger space in a better location, and then we will begin to use our great French Line [and Messageries Maritimes, the second of the French passenger lines] archives and collections. We want to create a tribute to all French passenger-ship companies, to the French merchant marine in general. It will be very special."

And so, quite happily for maritime historians and ocean-liner enthusiasts everywhere, those intricately detailed models, the glistening Lalique, the polished silver, the commemorative paintings, and those timeless photographs will see the light of day.

WILLIAM H. MILLER, JR.

INTRODUCTION

It is both an honor and a pleasure to be asked to contribute this introduction for Bill Miller's latest book, *Picture History of the French Line*, which I am sure will be a delight to ship lovers everywhere.

My association with that company began in 1956, when, having completed two years in the Royal Air Force, I sought employment with a shipping line. I had had an interest in passenger ships since the age of eleven, when I traveled by sea to Colombo, Ceylon (now Sri Lanka). I was offered a job in the London office of the French Line, on Cockspur Street, but at the time I did not realize just how fortunate I was. For the next eighteen years, until the office closed, I was able to indulge a rewarding hobby that was so full of highlights and pleasures it never seemed like work.

The Atlantic run was then peppered with outstanding liners, and the *Ile de France* and the *Liberté* were well up on the popularity list. Then there were the *Colombie*, the *Antilles*, and the *Flandre* operating to the West Indies. It was a busy time, with two or three arrivals and departures a week at Southampton. But the first six years were just the hors d'oeuvre; the main course arrived with the advent of the *France* in 1962.

My introduction to this great superliner was at the docking trials at Southampton, and this was followed over the years by a number of transatlantic voyages in both first and tourist class. She was a beautiful ship. Not since the *Normandie* had anyone seen such splendor as the first-class dining salon, with its imposing staircase; the magnificent theater, situated on two decks; and the superb promenade deck, completely given over to tourist-class passengers. The individually named suites in first class, much sought after by the rich and famous throughout the ship's North Atlantic and cruising career, took your breath away.

The success of the French Line resulted from its unparalleled level of service to its passengers. The *France* was the last of a long line of outstanding passenger ships to inherit the magic of what was indeed "France afloat." She continued the tradition. From the chief purser to the smartly red-uniformed "mousse" running messages, everyone contributed to the wonderful joie de vivre that permeated all the ships operated by the Compagnie Générale Transatlantique, the French Line. That spirited tradition is revivified in this superb photographic tribute.

BRIAN CHAPPELL

1. SAILS, PADDLE WHEELS, AND STEAM

The first French-owned transatlantic steamship service actually started in 1847 (seven years after Cunard, for example, and eight before the Hamburg-America Line) but was soon a financial flop. A second attempt in 1856 foundered as well. Meanwhile two brothers, Émile and Isaac Pereire, had formed the Compagnie Générale Maritime in February 1855 with a capital of 30 million French francs (or just over £1 million at the time). Their goal was to enter Atlantic service eventually. They soon acquired a Normandy-based firm that included no less than twenty-seven sailing ships and two small, 280-ton steamers. These last two ships had already been in Atlantic service, working the supply route to the fishing stations at French-owned St. Pierre and Miquelon, off Newfoundland. But great expansion came quickly. Within a year the CGM, as it was called, had seventy-six ships sailing out of Le Havre as well as Bordeaux to ports as far away as Australia, Madagascar, the West Indies, Mexico, Argentina, Chile, Peru, California, and, later, Algeria. But Atlantic passenger and mail service remained the Pereires' primary goal. In 1858, with the backing of the Rothschild family, plans were laid for five steamers for the New York run as well as seven for West Indies service. Mail subsidies were guaranteed by the French government.

There were some financial setbacks until, in 1861, the government advanced the necessary loans. Soon after, the company's name was changed to Compagnie Générale Transatlantique (CGT). Operations were reorganized under the watchful eye of Parisian administrators, certain unprofitable routes were discarded, and sailing ships were decreed to be elements of the past (the CGT did, in fact, have sailing ships in its fleet for at least another decade, until 1873). The new transatlantic service to New York was scheduled to start in the summer of 1864, but the French expedition to Mexico in 1861 prompted a speedup in planning. The 1,900-ton *Louisiane*, flying the CGT banner, sailed from St.-Nazaire to Veracruz in April 1862.

The French government had hoped to see the new fleet of eleven "large steamers" built in French yards, within three years. This was a mere fantasy; six had to be built abroad, in Scotland and England. The British charged the French £121,000 for each 3,400-ton ship. The first to be ready was the Greenock-built *Washington*, which set off from Le Havre for New York in June 1864. She was followed by the *Lafayette* and then by the *Europe*. Calls at Brest were soon introduced. By 1867 sailings were run fortnightly in each direction.

Still unable to find suitable French shipbuilders, the CGT, with fierce government prompting and backing, was determined to establish a shipyard of its own. The firm bought a strip of land at the mouth of the Loire at St.-Nazaire, in an area known locally as Penhoet. Drawing on craftsmen and expertise from shipbuilders in Scotland, the CGT built four slipways, enabling the French to build passenger ships of their own. The first of these was laid down in October 1862 as the *Atlantique* but was renamed *Impératrice Eugénie* by the time of launching, in April 1864. She went on the Mexico run.

CGT services prospered, and soon larger, better ships were added. By 1870 the New York–Le Havre crossing was being made in eight and a half days. Unlike most Atlantic steamers of their day, however, the CGT ships carried very little steerage, relying mainly on first- and second-class passengers. By 1872 paddle wheels had given way completely to steam propulsion. But a string of groundings, collisions, and even sinkings soon cast a pall over the emergent CGT. To regain public confidence, in 1876 the CGT advertised the use of "lighthouse [warning lights] and electric light" to minimize the risk of collision. A year later they boasted of "potent fog horns." In fact, the CGT's *Amérique* of 1876 was the first electrically lighted steamer on the Atlantic (and quite possibly in the world). Good fortune followed when, in 1879, the company received the government's mail contract for service between Marseilles, Algiers, and Tunis.

By 1891 the CGT's flourishing fortunes were reflected in the 9,047-ton *La Touraine;* the fifth-largest ship afloat and one of the fastest (with an average speed of 19 knots), she was renowned for her comfort and culinary excellence. The French soon capitalized on their fine image. By 1895 the CGT could advertise a sailing from Le Havre to New York or vice versa every Saturday throughout the year.

Renewals of the prized, lucrative government mail contracts demanded ever larger and faster ships. And so by 1899–1900, we see the addition of *La Lorraine* and *La Savoie*, each 11,100 tons and each capable of 20 knots. But although these two ships were built at the St.-Nazaire yard, company directors saw such a facility, with its five thousand workers, as a liability. Accordingly, it was sold off to private owners in 1900.

A new, more expansionist and progressive management that took over in 1904 spurred the building of seventeen ships between 1905 and 1911. The most important of these was the 13,700-ton *La Provence*, completed in 1906 and delivered with a trial speed of 23 knots, which made her one of the fastest ships afloat. She reached New York in just over six days. But an even bigger ship was soon on the boards, *La Picardie*. Weighing 23,600 tons and capped by four funnels—the ultimate symbols of transatlantic might, power, and prestige—she was the culmination of the CGT's first fifty years. But when she slipped down the ways at St.-Nazaire on a late-summer day in 1910, her name had been changed. She was christened the *France* and became the ultimate national symbol, France's very own floating palace, inaugurating a succession of some of the most spectacular ocean liners ever built.

WASHINGTON (above)

In 1861, when the CGT ordered its first brand-new Atlantic steamer, it still held that the paddle wheel was essential to high speed and sound performance. But in fact, the transoceanic paddler was already doomed. Screw ships were the proven and tested future. Cunard, that formidable rival from across the channel, had commissioned its last paddle-wheel ship, the *Scotia*, in 1862. And so France's first steamer for service to the United States, the *Washington*, was already outdated upon completion in June 1864.

An otherwise successful ship, she was converted within four years, by 1868, into a twin-screw ship at a Glasgow shipyard. She was fitted with new two-cylinder, single-expansion engines. Later used on the Brest–New York run, she spent her final years on the Le Havre–West Indies route. At age thirty-five, she was sold in 1899 and then scrapped at Marseilles a year later. [Built by Scott's Shipbuilding & Engineering Company, Greenock, Scotland, 1864. 3,401 gross tons; 345 feet long; 43 feet wide. Paddle wheels (later twin screw). Service speed 12.5 knots. 211 passengers (128 first class, 54 second class, 29 third class).]

LA CHAMPAGNE (opposite top)

Within twenty years the French were serious players on the fiercely competitive North Atlantic run. By this time their greatest rivals were the Germans, namely the Hamburg-America Line and the North German Lloyd. The latter company had just completed their *Aller* class of passenger ships, the first transatlantic liners with triple-expansion steam engines. At 5,200 tons, the *Aller* could travel at up to 17 knots. The French responded with the larger *La Champagne* class, at 6,700 tons and slightly higher speeds of 17.5 knots. Her three sisters were the *La Bretagne*, *La Bourgogne*, and *La Gascogne*. These ships also had the greatest capacities yet for French Line ships, approximately one thousand in all, mostly in steerage. However, while steerage–third class was the most profitable business for almost all Atlantic companies at this time, it was not a particularly strong consideration for the French. Quite simply, there were far fewer immigrants leaving France. (Third class became more significant to the French Line in the early twenties, especially because greater numbers wanted to leave a war-torn Europe and because competitors like the Germans were temporarily off the Atlantic sea-lanes in the wake of their defeat.)

Introduced in May 1886, *La Champagne* had an interesting career. In August 1887 she was seriously damaged in a collision with another French ship, the *Rio de Janeiro* of Chargeurs Réunis, just outside Le Havre (the latter ship sank). In 1896 she was extensively refitted with new quadruple-expansion engines and added space for 1,500 in steerage. Two years later, in 1898, she fractured her propeller shaft in the western Atlantic and was adrift for a time. She was later taken in tow by the Warren Line's *Roman* and brought into Halifax. Afterward she went on the Le Havre–Mexico service and still later on the Le Havre–Panama run. Early in World War I, in May 1915, she stranded at St.-Nazaire, broke her back, and was declared a complete wreck. [Built by Compagnie Générale Transatlantique, St.-Nazaire, France, 1886. 7,087 gross tons; 508 feet long; 51 feet wide. Compound engines, single screw. Service speed 17.5 knots. 1,055 passengers (390 first class, 65 second class, 600 steerage).]

LA TOURAINE (opposite bottom)

Completed in June 1891, *La Touraine* is remembered as one of the North Atlantic's most beautiful liners. Sleek lines, twin masts, and widely spaced short funnels suggested a large yacht. She was known to behave splendidly in rough weather and was the largest ship on the Le Havre–New York run when new. In 1900 her passage time between Le Havre and New York's Ambrose Light was six days, twenty-one hours. She was damaged in a very serious fire at Le Havre in January 1903, and her grand staircase (*page 4*), first-class dining saloon, and deluxe first-class cabins had to be rebuilt. She returned to service better than ever. The French Line avoided abnormal size or outstanding speed (the British had their record-breaking 32,000-ton sisters *Lusitania* and *Mauretania* underway by 1905, for example), instead mining the French reputation for elegant living, even at sea. Haute cuisine and luxury suites became recognized features of the French. On-board service was said to be flawless, the envy of almost all other Atlantic liner companies. The company trumpeted its slogan: "You are in France the moment you cross the gangplank!" It also merged first and second class and created the term "cabin class." Previously cabin class had been associated with old, outmoded steamers. *La Touraine* joined such ships as the new *Chicago* and the *Rochambeau* and herself became a "cabin steamer" in 1910. Two years later she made some special Canadian voyages, among these a passage between Halifax and Le Havre in five days and twenty-one hours. She was an armed merchant cruiser and then a trooper during World War I. Sold in 1922, she became a floating hotel for the Göteborg Exhibition in Sweden. She was scrapped at Dunkirk in 1924. [Built by Chantiers de Penhoet, St.-Nazaire, France, 1891. 9,047 gross tons; 536 feet long; 56 feet wide. Steam triple-expansion engines, twin screw. Service speed 19 knots. 1,090 passengers (392 first class, 98 second class, 600 third class).]

LA SAVOIE

La Savoie and her twin sister, *La Lorraine*, were not only the largest CGT liners by the turn of the century but also the company's first to boast of deluxe suites in first class. These accommodations had bedrooms, dressing and trunk rooms, a sitting room, and a full bathroom. *La Lorraine* made 22.5 knots during her sea trials, while *La Savoie* made the run to New York in six days, nine hours, at an average of 20.5 knots.

Shown (*above*) leaving New York and outbound along the Hudson River, with the piers of Hoboken, New Jersey, in the background, *La Savoie* later served (1914–18) as an armed merchant cruiser before resuming Le Havre–New York service. Replaced by the *Ile de France* in 1927, she went to the breakers at Dunkirk a year later. [Built by Compagnie Générale Transatlantique, St.-Nazaire, France, 1900. 11,168 gross tons; 580 feet long; 60 feet wide. Steam triple-expansion engines, twin screw. Service speed 21 knots. 953 passengers (437 first class, 118 second class, 398 third class).]

The dining room (*below*) aboard *La Savoie* was as famous for its beautiful decor as for its superb cuisine.

ROCHAMBEAU (above)

The *Rochambeau*, completed in September 1911, was among the first of the French Line's highly popular cabin steamers, accommodating 428 in cabin class—a comfortable but less expensive version of first class merged with second class—and 1,600 in third class. Used almost continuously on the New York run, she became a victim of the Depression in the early thirties. She ran her last crossing in July 1933 and was sold to Dunkirk scrappers a year later.

Named for the Comte de Rochambeau, who headed six thousand French troops during America's Revolutionary War, the *Rochambeau*, escorted by spraying fireboats, is shown above leaving Boston on a special sailing in May 1930. She is carrying 450 religious pilgrims from New England and other Eastern states who are bound for Africa to attend the Eucharistic Congress at Carthage. Boston's Mayor Curley bids them farewell from the launch just to the right of center. [Built by Chantiers de Penhoet, St.-Nazaire, France, 1911. 12,678 gross tons; 598 feet long; 63 feet wide. Steam triple-expansion engines, twin screw. Service speed 15 knots. 2,028 passengers (428 cabin class, 1,600 third class).]

A portrait of the Comte de Rochambeau hangs on the right in this view (*left*) of the cabin-class entrance hall aboard the *Rochambeau*.

LAFAYETTE/MEXIQUE (opposite)

Launched as the *Isle de Cuba* in May 1914 for the Le Havre–West Indies run, this ship was completed in October 1915 as the *Lafayette* for the New York service instead. She was then urgently needed to replace war losses and to assist with the movement of troops and special passengers; for a short time, in early 1917, she even served as a hospital ship. She resumed regular sailings in November 1919 until moved into the Caribbean trade in 1924. Four years later she was renamed *Mexique* and was assigned to the Le Havre–Veracruz service. She was called back to New York for one additional voyage, in September 1929, as a temporary replacement for the much larger *Paris*, which was undergoing extensive repairs following a fire. The *Mexique* was an early casualty of the Second World War. She was sunk soon after the Nazi invasion of France by a mine at Le Verdon on the river Gironde on June 19, 1940. [Built by Chantiers & Ateliers de Provence, Port de Bouc, France, 1915. 11,953 gross tons; 563 feet long; 64 feet wide. Steam triple-expansion engines, quadruple screw. Service speed 18 knots. 1,250 passengers (336 first class, 110 second class, 90 third class, 714 steerage).]

These superb photographs of the *Mexique*'s first-class library (*opposite top*) and restaurant (*opposite bottom right*) were taken during her final New York visit in 1929.

LEOPOLDINA/SUFFREN (above)

This ship came secondhand to the French. She had been North German Lloyd's *Blücher* and, while being used on the run from Bremerhaven to the east coast of South America, was seized in 1917, when Brazil declared war on Germany. She was renamed *Leopoldina* by the Brazilian government and then later, in April 1921, was chartered to the French Line to assist on the Le Havre–New York run. By this time, however, her original capacity of some 1,200 in three classes had been reduced to 750 in two classes, and she became another of the French Line's popular cabin steamers. Bought outright by the CGT in 1923, she was renamed *Suffern*. She was finally broken up in Italy in 1929. [Built by Blohm & Voss Shipbuilders, Hamburg, Germany, 1901. 12,350 gross tons; 550 feet long; 62 feet wide. Steam quadruple-expansion engines, twin screw. Service speed 16 knots. 750 passengers (500 cabin class, 250 third class).]

FLANDRE (1914) (below)

Smaller, combination passenger-cargo ships like the *Flandre* were built especially for the colonial West Indies and Central American trades of the CGT. The *Flandre* carried the all-important mails and supplies as well as the civil servants, the teachers, the missionaries, and the colonial administrators and their entourages. She also called at Vigo, in northern Spain, where she took on migrant workers and their families in her third-class quarters. Laid up at the onset of World War II, she was another early casualty, sunk by a magnetic mine in the river Gironde in September 1940. [Built by Chantiers de l'Atlantique, St.-Nazaire, France, 1914. 8,503 gross tons; 480 feet long; 57 feet wide. Quadruple-expansion engines, quadruple screw. Service speed 17 knots. 600 passengers in four classes.]

FRANCE (1912)

The *France* was quickly well established on the Atlantic circuit and was noted not only for her magnificent decor but also for her superb cuisine. Her first-class quarters were soon favored by the transatlantic social set, those millionaires and aristocrats who ferried to and from Europe and America. Below deck her westbound crossings were often booked to capacity with a full eight hundred in steerage. Her overall success (marred only by the need to change her propellers within a year to improve her speed) convinced the French to build even larger liners. [Built by Chantiers de Penhoet, St.-Nazaire, France, 1912. 23,666 gross tons; 713 feet long; 75 feet wide. Steam turbines, quadruple screw. Service speed 24 knots. 2,026 passengers (534 first class, 442 second class, 250 third class, 800 steerage).]

The *France* departed from Le Havre on her maiden voyage to New York on April 20, 1912, just five days after the *Titanic* tragedy. Once at Manhattan, she put into Pier 57, at the foot of West Fourteenth Street, a berth very near to the one that would have been used by the ill-fated White Star liner. The French were more than grateful that their new flagship, unlike the *Titanic*, carried enough lifeboats. This view (*below right*) of the *France*'s starboard side dates from 1929.

While her decor made her one of the most luxurious liners of her time, the *France* was also the first turbine-driven liner under the tricolor. She also had an auxiliary engine room abaft the main engine room. With four four-bladed propellers, each nearly 13 feet in diameter, she was intended to do as much as 25 knots (24 was her actual service speed as against, for example, the 21 knots of the much larger *Titanic*, which was completed at Belfast in the same year). The *France*'s coal bunkers had a capacity of 5,045 tons, allowing for a daily consumption of 680 to 720 tons. She is seen here (*below left*) on the Hudson as she approaches her West Side pier on July 5, 1924.

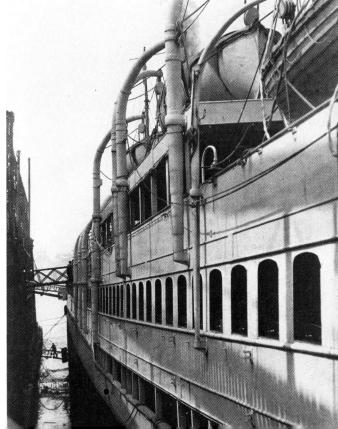

67678.

When World War I erupted in the summer of 1914, the *France* was temporarily laid up at Brest for safety. However, her value as an Allied trooper was quickly realized, and so she was transferred to the French government, renamed *France IV*, and sent off to the Dardanelles. In November 1915 she was converted at Toulon into a hospital ship, complete with an all-white hull and vivid Red Cross markings. Her lavish public rooms, such as the Salon Mixte in first class (*above*), were converted into hospital wards and surgeries. She handled tens of thousands of wounded servicemen over the next two years before she reverted to trooping in 1917. A year later she began returning American doughboys to New York and in 1919 worked a temporary, austerity-style Brest–New York service. She returned to Le Havre in August of that year, formally reestablishing the French Line's Le Havre run.

The *France*'s reputation was reestablished during the 1920s and included the fond dubbing of the liner as the "Chateau of the Atlantic." Between October 1923 and May 1924, during a very extensive refit at the St.-Nazaire yard, she was converted from coal to oil fuel. This was in keeping with almost all other Atlantic liners. Her accommodations were improved and modernized; steerage was reduced from 800 to a mere 152, reflecting the recent American immigration restrictions. But public rooms such as the magnificent first-class restaurant, a very impressive Louis XIV creation, remained. It had introduced the shipboard grand stairwell (*left*), which offered beautifully dressed, bejeweled ladies in particular the opportunity to make a stunning entrance. The second view (*opposite below*) shows the lower level of the same restaurant, where the menus remained beyond compare.

The *France*'s elegant Salon Louis XIV (*opposite top*) clearly had the style that many seasoned travelers said made her the best-decorated liner on the North Atlantic in the years just before World War I. Note the ornate ceiling, gilded columns, domed skylight, and fireplace at the far end, all overseen by a large portrait of the Sun King himself.

The *France* (seen above from the westbound *Paris* in the midtwenties) did meet with some misfortune in her later years. In June 1928 she hit a wreck in the Hudson River and seriously damaged her propellers. Despite speedy repairs, her future was cast into doubt by the onset of the Depression. Noticeably surpassed in style by such ships as the new *Ile de France*, by 1929–30 the aging *France* was sent off on periodic cruises to the West Indies, the Mediterranean, and the Norwegian fjords.

With the onset of the Great Depression, the *France*'s cruise sailings became an essential alternative to the declining Atlantic trade, which dropped from a million travelers in 1930 to half that number within five years. She proved especially popular in longer, more expensive cruises, with a mere two or three hundred millionaires on board. Her reputation as a rather notorious roller at sea hardly seemed to matter. Her kitchens were still outstanding, and her accommodations were superbly maintained, even if they were a bit dated by the sleek new standards of the early thirties. Even her external design was in marked contrast, as is evident in the photograph below as she approaches New York's Narrows on April 22, 1930. On the left is the new German *Bremen*, a 51,000-tonner that was then the Atlantic's fastest liner, noted for her long, slender, almost squat appearance (in fact, her two stacks were soon made higher because of continual smoke and soot problems).

The *France* completed her last French Line sailing in the summer of 1932 and was laid up, presumably until better times. But a year later she had a fire, one which greatly reduced her chances of returning to service. In late 1934 she was sold to Dunkirk scrappers and then left Le Havre under tow, on April 15, 1935, just weeks before the maiden sailing of a newer, far larger French flagship, the 79,000-ton *Normandie*.

2. SIZE, LUXURY, AND STYLE

As the first steel plates were laid in place at St.-Nazaire for the new French Line flagship, its first and only four-stacker, the first decade of the new century was drawing to a close. For transatlantic passenger shipping those ten years had seen epochal changes. Business was booming: in 1907 alone twelve thousand steerage passengers were arriving in New York harbor each day from places like Göteborg, Antwerp, Hamburg, Liverpool, Naples, and Fiume. And regular traffic in first and second class had increased as well. The battle to produce the most luxurious first-class accommodation was as fervent as ever. Every steamer company wanted its share—and a very profitable share it was.

It was a decade of rapid technological advances. In 1900 the Hamburg-America Line's 16,500-ton, 22-knot *Deutschland* was not only the fastest ship afloat but one of the largest. By 1910 plans had been drawn for the first 50,000-tonner, another Hamburg-America ship, in fact, the *Imperator*. By then Cunard's *Mauretania* was firmly entrenched as the Blue Ribband (speed) champion, with a record of more than 26 knots. Along with the *Lusitania*, the Cunard Company was planning a third, even larger ship, the 45,000-ton *Aquitania*. Cunard's closest rival, the White Star Line, had three behemoths in the works—the 46,000-ton sisters *Olympic* and *Titanic* and the 48,000-ton *Gigantic*, which soon became the *Britannic*. France responded with the *France*, a far smaller ship at 23,000 tons but nonetheless considered a superliner, one of the floating palaces of the Edwardian era. From her towering mast the tricolor flew proudly when she went into service in the spring of 1912, just days after the immortal *Titanic* plunged to the bottom of the western Atlantic.

But as benefactor, catalyst, even instigator, the French government wanted more. National prestige was important—"the glory of France" had to be proudly represented on the most important ocean run anywhere: the North Atlantic. The French wanted to join Britain and Germany in that elite club of passenger-ship supremacy. Parisian ministers created a new mail and subsidy agreement, one that called for four large liners, perhaps even one every four years.

The next step up for France was the 34,500-ton *Paris*, whose construction was begun in 1913 but then halted a year later as the war started. She was, in fact, quietly launched in 1916, but then the unfinished hull was sent off to a secluded anchorage for the duration of the hostilities. When she finally emerged in the summer of 1921, the French could not have been more pleased. With her excellent speed and her imposing but decorous stature, she was without peer on the Atlantic. And few ships proved a better investment. Her opulent first-class quarters were so popular that year after year the *Paris* crossed the Atlantic with the lowest percentage of vacant berths of all major liners.

But as ocean travel moderated in the 1920s, many pronounced the end of the age of the big, important, luxury-filled liner. According to some pundits, smaller ships, 25,000 tons or less, were the future. But the French Line directors disagreed, unveiling plans for an even more stunning and sumptuous ship: the 43,000-ton *Ile de France*. Innovative, stylish, trend-setting, luxuriously appealing, and, of course, gastronomically sublime, she was perhaps the most successful and most beloved liner ever owned by the CGT.

PARIS

The *Paris* was one of the finest, best-decorated, and most luxurious liners ever to sail the North Atlantic. She was an interwar ship, finished at the end of World War I and destroyed just before World War II. She was an immediate follow-up to the great success of the 23,600-ton *France* of 1912. Her design was reworked and enlarged at the Penhoet shipyards. The refinements and alterations included a larger three-funnel design and a forward-looking aesthetic. The gilded Louis XIV of the earlier liners gave way to a more startling art nouveau, even primitive art deco, on the new vessel.

The French Line planned to introduce the *Paris* in 1915 and then, in rapid sequence, two additional liners: the *Ile de France* in 1920 and the *Lafayette* by 1925. But the war interrupted this ambitious plan, halting construction of the *Paris* and leaving her idle for five years. She was quietly launched in 1916, but only to free the shipyard slipway for more urgent military work. Work on the ship did not resume until 1919–20. The French Line's whole schedule of new liners was altered, pushing scheduled launch of the *Ile de France* to 1926 or 1927 and that of the *Lafayette* to 1929–30.

After a successful series of trials and glowing press reports about her "new-generation" interiors, in June 1921 the new *Paris* sailed on her maiden voyage to New York. Thereafter she called at Southampton in both direc-

tions on her year-round relays to and from Le Havre. In 1922, after an absence of nearly forty-four years, she and the *France* reintroduced a French call at Plymouth (which replaced Southampton) in England's West Country. Soon even the smaller West Indies–routed ships called there as well.

In this outbound view (*above*) of the *Paris* from the midthirties, three of what were then the world's tallest office towers are behind her. The Woolworth Tower (then sixth largest) is just to the right of her third funnel; the Bank of Manhattan Building (fourth largest) is behind the foremast; and the Cities Service Tower (third largest), with the tiered rooftop, is just to the left of the bow. [Built by Chantiers de l'Atlantique, St.-Nazaire, France, 1921. 34,569 gross tons; 764 feet long; 85 feet wide. Steam turbines, quadruple screw. Service speed 22 knots. 1,930 passengers (560 first class, 530 second class, 840 third class).]

New York's Pier 57, built in 1908–09, was said by the French Line to be "the gateway to all of Europe." It was used by the French Line until 1935, when the first arrival of the giant *Normandie* prompted a move north to Pier 88, at West Forty-eighth Street. Pier 57 was at West Fourteenth Street in the city's Chelsea section. In this view (*below*) from the late twenties, three French liners are in port together: (from left to right) the *De Grasse*, the *Paris*, and, at adjacent Pier 58, the *Suffren*. On the far left is the stern section of Cunard's *Franconia*.

A midthirties description of the *Paris*'s highlights reads as follows:

> The Promenade Deck is enclosed with glass screens for the whole of its
> length and is brought out slightly on each side. It is also rubber tiled to
> deaden sound and prevent slipping. Other rooms on this deck besides the
> Main Smoking Room are the "Salon de Thé," where "moderne" is the
> style and which is supplemented by light-colored walls, indirect lighting
> and a large skylight. In the center of this room is one of the finest
> achievements of the *Paris*'s decoration, namely the illuminated dance
> floor, where frosted glass panels in the actual floor are illuminated from
> beneath by lights, giving a very pleasing effect. Next is the Balcony of the
> Main Foyer. Then, there is the Grand Salon, in the style of the time of
> Marie Antoinette, yet in a modern way. It has a large dome, the topmost
> part of which is glass, as well as large windows and mirrors. At one end is
> the library, where books in both French and English can be found.

The photograph above shows the Salon Mixte.

The main dining room (*right*) on the *Paris* was located on C deck. A large
stairway led to the Balcony Dining Salon. The room itself was supported by
square pillars, over which a large glass dome formed a central nave with an
aisle on each side, both upstairs and downstairs. Halfway up the staircase at
the end of this room was an array of magnificent mirrors that reflected both
the light and the colors of this wonderful room. There were 130 tables in
all, most of which sat four.

The *Paris* did suffer an unusual number of mishaps. On October 15, 1927, she rammed and sank the freighter *Bessengen* in Lower New York Bay. Six perished. On April 6, 1929, she went aground (*above*), again in Lower New York Bay. Her pilot was said to have misjudged in thick fog. Then, less than two weeks later, on April 18, she was aground again, this time off England's Eddystone Light. But far worse problems lay ahead. Four months later, on August 20, she was almost completely destroyed by fire while docked at Le Havre. The blaze began in her third-class section, spread to second class, and finally reached the lavish first class. Initial reports were that the eight-year-old ship might have to be scrapped. However, within five months she was repaired, restored, and even modernized at St.-Nazaire.

The *Paris* (shown at right being repaired at Rotterdam in April 1929) was also affected by the declining passenger loads on the Atlantic of the early thirties. In a search for alternative revenues, she was, like the older *France*, often sent on all-first-class cruises. In the winter of 1931, for example, she departed on her first Mediterranean trip, which called at Tenerife, Casablanca, Gibraltar, Algiers, Naples, Corsica, Monte Carlo, Cannes, Majorca, and the Azores. Priced from just over $16 a day, the fares included the option of leaving the ship on the French Riviera and then traveling by train for a stay in Paris and then onward to Le Havre for a return to New York on the *Ile de France*.

In 1935, as the *Normandie* was coming into service, the CGT planned to convert the *Paris* into a full-time cruise ship. With a swimming pool added to her aft decks, she would even be redone with a tropical, all-white hull. But this never came to pass. Instead, she continued to divide her schedules between crossings and cruises.

At Le Havre on April 19, 1939, the *Paris* was being loaded with French art treasures bound for display at the New York World's Fair when fire broke out and spread quickly. Smoke poured from her top decks and windows, with the *Champlain* just ahead and the *Normandie* behind in the huge graving dock. Fire fighters were summoned immediately and inadvertently administered the coup de grace by loading her with too much water. After burning through the night, the blistered *Paris* capsized, with less than a quarter of her starboard side poking above local waters. She was a complete loss. Almost the same day her two tall masts had to be cut so that the giant *Normandie* could be moved out of her repair slip. Little else was done to the *Paris*, however, especially since insurance underwriters hovered about her remains for months. When World War II started less than five months later, any plans for salvage were forgotten.

In 1944, during the heavy bombings of Le Havre, the *Paris* was damaged even further. She was still left untouched after the war ended. Then, in November 1946, when the former German superliner *Europa* was brought to Le Havre to become the French *Liberté*, that 49,000-ton ship was ripped from her moorings by an Atlantic gale and slammed into the wreckage of the *Paris*. Although the larger ship was holed, it settled upright and could be saved. But harbor officials finally realized that the remains of the *Paris* were a menace and in 1947 had her dismantled where she lay.

ILE DE FRANCE

The *Ile de France* was the first large liner designed and built after World War I. At the time of her construction, the Paris offices of the French Line predicted that she would be the most magnificent liner on the North Atlantic. She was not intended, however, to be the biggest or the fastest or the most notable in any way (the largest at the time was the 56,000-ton *Majestic* of the White Star Line, and the Blue Ribband for speed was still held by Cunard's *Mauretania*). Even her appearance, while pleasant, was modeled on that of her forebears, especially the *Paris*. She had three evenly raked funnels and two tall masts. But the French Line's excitement focused on her interiors, which were revolutionary. She was boldly modern, certainly unlike anything yet seen on the Atlantic. She was an individual with a style of her own, a revolutionary, a trend setter, the pioneer of ocean-liner style of design. The architects and designers and decorators of the *Ile de France* did not copy traditional shoreside themes (such as manor houses, palaces, even Moorish concoctions) but created the first true floating luxury resort, a moving hotel. As the French Line president said at the time, "To live is not to copy."

In this 1930 view (*above*), a catapult for a seaplane is affixed to the stern of the *Ile de France*. It was used to launch such planes, which were loaded with mail, prior to reaching New York or Le Havre. This meant something close to a twenty-four-hour advance in delivery. Other lines that for a time had this feature were the American superliner *Leviathan* and the two new German record breakers, the *Bremen* and the *Europa*. [Built by Chantiers de l'Atlantique, St.-Nazaire, France, 1927. 43,153 gross tons; 791 feet long; 91 feet wide; 34-foot draft. Steam turbines, quadruple screw. Service speed 23.5 knots. 1,786 passengers (537 first class, 603 second class, 646 third class).]

The *Ile de France* was launched on March 14, 1926, at the Penhoet shipyards in the presence of thousands of government and company officials, workers, their families, and general spectators. Fourteen months later, on May 29, she left the builder's yard for her sea trials, which resulted in a very pleasing 23.5 knots as her top speed. She returned for a brief survey at Brest and then sailed to Le Havre, her home port, where she docked on June 5. Once she was opened for public inspection, thousands of visitors, particularly the press, were ecstatic in their praise of her luxury and novelty.

On June 22, 1927, she sailed from Le Havre, made a brief stop at Plymouth on the following day, and then proceeded to New York for a gala maiden welcome. She is shown (*left*) at Pier 57 during her extended maiden visit. Within her first decade, she was one of the Atlantic's most popular liners, averaging an impressive (especially in the Depression years) 795 passengers on each crossing. She was described as "the cheeriest way to cross the North Atlantic" and as "a bit of mainland France herself."

In another maiden-voyage view at Pier 57, the advances in ship construction and size are quite evident: the 43,000-ton *Ile de France* compared with the 11,000-ton *La Savoie*, built twenty-seven years earlier, in 1900.

The accommodations on board the new *Ile de France* were divided into three classes: first class, cabin class, and third class. But all cabins, even those in third class, had beds instead of bunks. First class contained a large assortment of suites and deluxe cabins and was acclaimed as offering the finest selection at sea. By 1935 the *Ile de France* had carried more first-class passengers than any other Atlantic liner.

Each of the *Ile de France*'s 390 first-class cabins was decorated in a different style. Her overall style was described as being more eclectic than modern. Each public room seemed unique as well. Overall, she introduced the age of art deco to the ocean liner through angular furniture, sweeping columns and panels, inventive lighting, and a great sense of spaciousness that replaced the cluttered feel of the liners of the past. The bar, for example, was supposedly the largest afloat. The main restaurant was also said to be the largest at sea in 1927 and rose three decks high. Like the *France* and then the *Paris*, it had a grand stairway as a main entrance. The grand foyer was three decks high, and the chapel was done in Gothic, with fourteen pillars. There was also a shooting gallery, a merry-go-round, and a well-equipped gymnasium.

The three big funnels on the *Ile de France* (*above*) were used as a symbol of the French Line and appeared on company literature as well as on the baggage tags that were attached to carryons, suitcases, and those vast trunks that were very much a part of transatlantic trade in the twenties and thirties.

One of the many sections of the vast boiler rooms aboard the *Ile de France* (*right*).

Celebrities from Hollywood, politics, industry, and European royalty were frequent passengers aboard the French liners in the twenties and thirties. In this view, in the winter of 1929–30, Maurice Chevalier (*top left*) is returning to his homeland aboard the *Paris*. Reporters have seen him off at Pier 57 just before sailing.

In 1933 the *Ile de France*, which was suffering from serious vibrations, was sent back to her builder's yard at St.-Nazaire (shown bottom left in one of the dry docks), where every piece of wood paneling was systematically removed, padded, and then reinserted. At the time, just across the dockyard, the 79,000-ton *Normandie* was nearing completion. Although still unnamed at the time, she was already being described as the "super *Ile de France*." She was, of course, even more innovative, more revolutionary, more dramatic.

In 1938 the *Ile de France* made news again. At New York she was towed by the new diesel-powered tugboat *Sheila Moran*. It was the first time that a single tug could tow a major Atlantic liner (*bottom right*).

At the outbreak of World War II in September 1939, the *Ile de France* was at New York's Pier 88, just opposite the great *Normandie* and, for a time, moored side by side with the *Champlain*. The French Line, fearing enemy advances, had no desire to send the ship back to her homeland (France fell to Germany the following spring). But the *Ile*, as she was often called, was occupying an important Manhattan berth and so, under the care of no fewer than ten tugs, was towed to Staten Island and laid up. Her staff of eight hundred was reduced to one hundred for maintenance and security. In the news item accompanying this nighttime view from March 22, 1940, it is already being rumored that she might soon be leaving for some secret war duty.

Finally put on loan to the British Admiralty, the *Ile* was loaded with war materials (including planes, shown above being loaded onto her aft deck by a floating crane) and, painted in gray and black, sailed on May 1 for Europe and then Singapore. Once in the East, she was more formally seized by the British government following the fall of France. She later served with an Asian crew under P&O management, but then, in 1943, trooped on the Atlantic under Cunard–White Star management, with a European staff.

3. OTHER SHIPS, OTHER ROUTES

Among the French liners the twenties and thirties seem to have been dominated by three ships: the smart *Paris*, the innovative *Ile de France*, and, most prominently, the exceptional *Normandie*. On the current nostalgia market they command the highest prices—a *Normandie* poster recently sold for $14,000, a 20-inch model of the *Paris* for $800, and a set of a dozen black-and-white *Ile de France* postcards for $200. Moreover, a video production company has produced a documentary on the Atlantic liner trade. Their interest in the French was rather limited: "As much as possible on the *Normandie* and maybe something on the *Ile de France*, but none of the others!"

The French Line and other French passenger companies built many impressive, interesting ships between 1920 and 1940. The CGT's *De Grasse* (1924) sailed not only to New York but also to the West Indies and as a cruise ship. The *Colombie* (1931) was aimed exclusively at the colonial Caribbean. The CGT also added tonnage to the North African service out of Marseilles.

In the wake of the stunning *Ile de France* of 1927, the company added two very fine cabin liners to the New York run: the 25,000-ton *Lafayette* in 1930 and then, two years later, the 28,000-ton *Champlain*. The latter was the more novel-looking ship and was clearly a prelude to the advanced design of the superliner that the CGT was planning for the midthirties. Both the *Lafayette* and the *Champlain* were also part of that government contract to build better, more efficient ships that would enhance the image of France itself.

Messageries Maritimes, based in Marseilles, had France's "second" passenger fleet. Its ships—with names like *Aramis*, *Explorateur Grandidier*, *Fontainebleau*, *Jean La Borde*, and *Sphinx*—worked largely colonial services: Indochina, Mauritius, French islands in the South Pacific. They also traded to the Far East, India, Australia, and the Middle East. Their splendid poster art hints at their exotic range: a moonlit liner at Saigon, a sunny passage through Suez, a ship moored off an Indian Ocean beach. Often exquisitely appointed within, Messageries Maritimes passenger vessels were also known to be rather eccentric on the outside. Its motor liner *Félix Roussel*, for example, had two very low square smokestacks.

Compagnie de Navigation Sud-Atlantique ran a luxury service out of Bordeaux across the South Atlantic to ports along the east coast of South America. They also produced one of the most spectacular liners of the thirties, now largely forgotten, the 42,000-ton *L'Atlantique*. Other lines, such as Chargeurs Réunis and Transports Maritimes, also traded to South America. Mostly colonial ports in Africa were served by Fabre, Fraissinet, Mixte, and Paquet. Just about all of these companies and their ships were interconnected (either through branch offices scattered across North America or by train connections from Le Havre) to the French Line itself.

DE GRASSE (1924)

While the French Line seems best remembered for such big liners of the twenties as the *Paris* and the *Ile de France*, plans for other, albeit smaller passenger ships included the *De Grasse*, a so-called intermediate liner, completed in 1924. She spent many years on the North Atlantic.

Ordered from British builders, Cammell Laird at Birkenhead, her first keel plates were laid soon after the First World War, in March 1920. Rumor was that she would be called the *Suffren*. But delays, work stoppages, and then material shortages delayed her launch for four years, until February 1924. She was named *De Grasse* at the time. Still more complications followed. After yet another shipyard strike at Birkenhead, the nearly complete liner was moved to St.-Nazaire for final fitting out. In the summer of 1924, she set out on her maiden crossing to New York (where she is shown above arriving in a later view, in 1927). [Built by Cammell, Laird & Company Limited, Birkenhead, England, 1924. 17,707 gross tons; 574 feet long; 71 feet wide. Steam turbines, twin screw. Service speed 16 knots. 2,111 passengers (399 cabin class, 1,712 third class).]

The *De Grasse* sailed mostly on the Le Havre–New York run but was occasionally sent, during the winter season, to the Caribbean from Le Havre. She was used more and more for cruising in the mid thirties and was laid up for a time following the appearance of the giant *Normandie* in 1935. A year later it was reported that she would be moved to the Pacific to sail to Tahiti, with connections from Australia and perhaps the U.S. West Coast. This never came to pass, however. In 1938 she was upgraded for more cruising duty with a new sun deck, an outdoor swimming pool, and a new two-deck-high restaurant. Her 1939 itineraries included a nine-day cruise from New York on April 7 for Miami, Nassau, and Havana. The minimum fare was $100. That summer, on July 24, she cruised from Le Havre to Scotland, Iceland, Spitsbergen, the North Cape, and the Norwegian fjords. Fares for this twenty-one-day cruise were priced in three classes: from f6,900 in first class, from f5,200 in tourist class, and f2,400 in special, economy class. This wide, partially enclosed promenade deck area (*below*) was a popular feature during these leisure voyages.

On October 16, 1939, the *De Grasse* arrived at New York's Pier 88 on a far less joyous occasion. She had crossed from Le Havre in complete secrecy, blacked out from stem to stern and sending no radio messages whatsoever. She carried 281 passengers being evacuated from war-struck Europe. Her portholes and windows had been painted over and her glass doors and skylights taped; she had so few lights left that passengers reported that it was difficult to read. She is shown above in company with two laid-up French liners: the *Ile de France* (left), temporarily at Pier 86, the former North German Lloyd berth; and two funnels of the *Normandie*, which remained on the north side of Pier 88 for some time to come.

The *De Grasse* returned to home waters later in 1939 and then was laid up at Bordeaux. She quickly fell into the hands of the Nazis, who left her in her moorings through the remaining war years, using it as an accommodation ship. In their retreat on August 30, 1944, the Germans deliberately scuttled her. She was salvaged exactly a year later.

LAFAYETTE (1929)

Launched in May 1929, the *Lafayette* (*below*) followed the *Ile de France* but was not a follow-up. Unlike the *Ile*, which was a larger, improved version of the *Paris*, the *Lafayette* was smaller, a motor liner aimed at the intermediate, cabin-class market. Her design was part of the new twenties style that followed the likes of Italy's *Saturnia* and *Vulcania*, the Dutch *Christiaan Huygens*, and Japan's *Chichibu Maru*. Like the *Lafayette*, they had long, low profiles topped by single, squat funnels. The *Lafayette* carried the design further by having her foremast placed above the wheelhouse.

After entering service in May 1930, the *Lafayette* ran regular Le Havre–Plymouth–New York crossings as well as many cruises. Sample leisure trips in the mid-1930s included a four-day cruise from Quebec City to New York, priced from $35; an eleven-day cruise from New York to Nassau, Kingston, Port-au-Prince, and Bermuda, priced from $110; and a seventeen-day cruise from New York to Fort de France, Trinidad, La Guaira, Cartagena, Cristobal, and Kingston, priced from $170. [Built by Chantiers de l'Atlantique, St.-Nazaire, France, 1930. 25,178 gross tons; 613 feet long; 77 feet wide. MAN diesels, twin screw. Service speed 17 knots. 1,079 passengers (583 cabin class, 388 tourist class, 108 third class).]

Internally the *Lafayette* was very much a decorative successor to the illustrious *Ile de France*. This new ship was done in modern, sleek art deco.

Her cabin-class restaurant, which is shown here, includes the grand stairwell as an entrance.

Altogether, the French lost four noted liners to fire within six years: *l'Atlantique* in 1933, the *Georges Philippar* that same year, the *Lafayette* in 1938, and finally the *Paris* a year later. The *Lafayette* was being overhauled in the large graving dock at Le Havre when she caught fire on May 4 (*above*). The fire started when an engineer was lighting one of the boiler furnaces, and the flames soon spread to the oil tanks. Fire fighters soon found it impossible to quell the blaze and allowed it to take its course. She was a complete loss and later was sold to ship breakers in Rotterdam.

CHAMPLAIN

The *Champlain* (shown at right in a 1933 New York departure from the stern section of the *De Grasse*) was a larger, improved version of the *Lafayette*, which arrived two years before her. But this newer ship was also more of a prelude to the French Line's superliner of the future, the glorious *Normandie*, due out in three years, in 1935. The *Champlain* had an especially modern look about her: a raked bow, uncluttered upper decks, and a rather distinctive single stack with a slanted, smoke-deflector top. Carrying little more than a thousand passengers at full capacity, she, too, was an intermediate liner aimed at periodic cruising to Bermuda, the Caribbean, eastern Canada, and more remote destinations: West Africa, the Mediterranean, and Northern Europe. [Built by Chantiers de l'Atlantique, St.-Nazaire, France, 1932. 28,124 gross tons; 641 feet long; 82 feet wide. Steam turbines, twin screw. Service speed 19 knots. 1,063 passengers (623 cabin class, 308 tourist class, 132 third class).]

Both the exterior and the interiors of the *Champlain* were a prelude to the exceptional stylings of the *Normandie*. Although smaller, slower, and far less renowned than that forthcoming flagship, the *Champlain* was certainly one of the most smartly decorated liners on the Atlantic in the thirties. The smoking room (*above*), for example, included a semicircular bar with glass etchings of vineyard scenes in France. It had pigskin walls with wooden pillars, on which were carved the emblems of playing cards. Rooms were illuminated by means of an indirect process, a notable design touch used by the French beginning with the *Ile de France* five years before. In front of the smoking room and behind a large foyer was the Grand Salon (*below*), which had parchment walls, large windows along each side, and lighting from large cylindrical stands along the walls. This room was dominated by a large painting of the explorer Samuel de Champlain.

On the promenade deck was the main foyer (*above left*), which was also used as an entertainment space. A well in the deck above formed a gallery. Adjoining this was the ship's library.

The dining room (*above right*) on board the *Champlain*, done in Spanish patio style, was 65 feet long and two decks high in the center. Ironwork was used along the upper walls and marble on the stairwells and in other areas. A large serving table was the centerpiece. The lighting was arranged through large rectangular panels in the ceiling.

Especially in cabin class, staterooms on board the *Champlain* were especially spacious. Many included private showers and toilets. The room below was priced at $260 per person in the peak summer season in 1935 for the eight-day passage from New York to Plymouth and Le Havre.

The newly heightened funnel on the *Champlain* is shown above in this late afternoon view, off Staten Island, New York. As on many other liners, the original low stack caused problems with smoke and soot along the aft passenger decks.

A mountainous North Atlantic wave seems to engulf the bow section of the *Champlain* as she steamed westward in heavy weather (*below left*). Delayed, she finally reached New York on January 26, 1939.

Laid up at Pier 88 when World War II started in September 1939, the *Champlain* was painted over in wartime gray (*below right*) and later re-turned to Le Havre. She made one more sailing, in April 1940, when she arrived at New York unannounced (as shown on the south side of Pier 88) carrying 420 passengers: 315 Jewish refugees from Central Europe and 105 Spanish refugees from internment camps in France. She returned to home waters soon afterward, where she struck a mine near La Pallice on June 17 and then quickly sank. Three hundred thirty people perished. The wreckage removal proceeded slowly, beginning in 1946 and ending eighteen years later.

COLOMBIE

Following the *Ile de France* (1927) and the *Lafayette* (1930) but just before the *Champlain* (1932), the French Line ordered its largest and finest liner for its Le Havre–Caribbean service: the *Colombie*, commissioned in the summer of 1931 and seen above at Le Havre from the deck of the arriving *Normandie* on July 5, 1937. [Built by Ateliers et Chantiers de France, Dunkirk, France, 1931. 13,391 gross tons; 508 feet long; 66 feet wide. Steam turbines, twin screw. Service speed 17 knots. 491 passengers (201 first class, 146 second class, 144 third class).]

Based at Le Havre, with service calls at Southampton and Plymouth, the *Colombie* traveled to the West Indies, mostly to Guadelupe and Martinique, occasionally calling at other ports such as Trinidad, Barbados, San Juan, and even French Guiana. This yachtlike ship was also sent cruising from Le Havre to the Norwegian fjords and Baltic cities, the Mediterranean, and West Africa. Her most unusual cruise was undoubtedly a transatlantic crossing to New York in August 1939, specially for the World's Fair. She is shown below at one of Manhattan's last peacetime gatherings of passenger ships along Luxury Liner Row on August 27. From top to bottom are the *Drottningholm* of the Swedish-American Line; the *Roma* of the Italian Line; the *Colombie* and the *De Grasse* of the French Line; and the *Hamburg* and the *St. Louis* of the Hamburg-America Line.

FELIX ROUSSEL

Messageries Maritimes, based at Marseilles, was France's second-largest passenger-ship company. It offered many services but was primarily interested in the colonial run via Suez to French Indochina and the Far East. It was heavily supported by government contracts, both for passengers and for cargo (especially the mails). Three of its finest liners were added in the early thirties. They were the *Félix Roussel* (*above*), the *Georges Philippar,* and the *Aramis*. Richly decorated within, particularly in their first-class quarters, these ships also had distinctive-looking exteriors: each had a set of low square funnels.

The *Félix Roussel* survived the Second World War and served with the French until 1955. She then became the transatlantic liner *Arosa Sun* for the Swiss-owned Arosa line before spending her last years, from 1960 until 1974, as an accommodation for a steel plant at IJmuiden in Holland. She was broken up in Spain in the summer of 1974. The *Georges Philippar* caught fire on her return maiden voyage, on May 16, 1932, in the Gulf of Aden. Fifty-four passengers perished, and the ship itself sank three days later. The *Aramis* was seized by the Japanese at Saigon in 1942 and became their transport *Teia Maru*. She was later sunk by an American submarine off the Philippines in August 1944. [Built by Ateliers et Chantiers de la Loire, St.-Nazaire, France, 1931. 17,539 gross tons; 567 feet long; 68 feet wide. Sulzer diesels, twin screw. Service speed 15 knots. 1,045 passengers (196 first class, 110 second class, 89 third class, 650 steerage).]

MARRAKECH

For its North African services to Algiers and Tunis from Marseilles, the French Line had a separate but rather extensive fleet of smaller passenger ships. Built originally as the *Haiti* for the Le Havre–West Indies run, this ship later became the *Marrakech* for the African trade (*opposite top*). Her career was rather remarkable, spanning forty-eight years. She was scrapped in 1951. [Built by Chantiers et Ateliers de Provence, Port Bouc, France, 1913. 6,288 gross tons; 410 feet long; 51 feet wide. Twin-screw, steam, triple-expansion engines. Service speed 13 knots. Approximately 600 passengers in four classes.]

L'ATLANTIQUE

She was called a "first cousin" to the exceptional *Ile de France*. She was by far the largest as well as the grandest liner ever used on the Europe–South America trade. With this ship the French Line, already acclaimed on the North Atlantic, had the competitive edge on the South Atlantic as well. Ordered from the same St.-Nazaire yards that had built the big French Line ships, she was launched, quite appropriately, as *l'Atlantique* (*opposite bottom*) on April 15, 1930. Her completion was scheduled for the following summer, in September 1931, with a maiden voyage from Bordeaux to Rio de Janeiro, Santos, Montevideo, and Buenos Aires. Her only shortcomings were the onset of the Depression and her external appearance—top-heavy and almost clumsy (later, in an effort to enhance her appearance, her three funnels were heightened).

Life for her was tragically brief. While on a voyage from Bordeaux to Le Havre on January 4, 1933, without passengers and with a reduced crew, she caught fire and burned off the Channel island of Guernsey. Nineteen seamen died in the blaze. Towed into Cherbourg two days later, she was abandoned by her owners as an economic loss and was handed over to the underwriters. Laid up at Cherbourg for three years while legal battles over her played out, she was finally sold to Glasgow ship breakers and delivered to them in February 1936. [Built by Chantiers de l'Atlantique, St.-Nazaire, France, 1931. 42,512 gross tons; 742 feet long; 92 feet wide. Steam turbines, quadruple screw. Service speed 21 knots. 1,156 passengers (414 first class, 158 second class, 584 third class).]

Le Paquebot "MARRAKECH", Cie Générale Transatlantique.

Le Paquebot « L'ATLANTIQUE »

L'Atlantique was the most splendid liner on the Europe–South America run in the early thirties. Shown here are the first-class main restaurant with grand stairwell (*above*), the smoking room (*below*), and the grand foyer and shopping arcade (*opposite top*).

PASTEUR

Ordered as a latter-day replacement for *l'Atlantique*, the *Pasteur* (*below* and *next page*) was built in the late thirties and was intended to be the fastest, most luxurious liner on the same Europe–South America trade. The French, namely the Compagnie de Navigation Sud-Atlantique, were keenly interested in outpacing all the existing competition, especially Germany's *Cap Arcona* and a new British entry, the *Andes* of the Royal Mail Lines. The new French ship was, in the end, slightly larger and more powerful and was sure to be the "crack ship" to South America.

During her trials in the summer of 1939, her turbines produced a highly satisfactory speed of 26 knots. Her maiden sailing, from Bordeaux to Rio de Janeiro, Santos, Montevideo, and Buenos Aires, was set for that September. But the start of World War II thwarted these plans. With her maiden trip canceled, she was sent to lay up at Brest, supposedly as a temporary measure. In June 1940, with Nazi forces close at hand, she was hurriedly ordered to Halifax. With a limited crew and no passengers, she carried a very valuable cargo: a large shipment of gold from the French National Reserves bound for wartime safe storage in Canada. Upon arrival she was transferred to the British and placed under the management of Cunard–White Star. She visited New York (where she is shown below outbound on the Hudson River) before she was ordered out to the Far East for trooping. Later in the war, in 1944–45, she sailed almost regularly on the North Atlantic, mostly in company with another large French liner, the famed *Ile de France*. [Built by Chantiers de l'Atlantique, St.-Nazaire, France, 1939. 29,253 gross tons; 697 feet long; 88 feet wide. Steam turbines, quadruple screw. Service speed 23 knots. 751 passengers (287 first class, 126 second class, 338 third class).]

4. PAQUEBOT EXTRAORDINAIRE: THE NORMANDIE

June 3, 1935, was unquestionably one of New York harbor's greatest days. Tugs, yachts, ferryboats, excursion steamers, and spraying fireboats were out in force. Special charter planes flew overhead, and a blimp hovered about; there was even a giant Mickey Mouse mounted on a barge. Flags waved and horns tooted and sirens blared and crowds cheered, applauded, and even wept at times. In the midst of the enduring Depression, "a great ray of sunlight," as one reporter called it, was coming from France, albeit two years behind schedule. Said to be the most spectacular liner of all time, the $60-million (more than $600 million in 1996 dollars) *Normandie* was arriving on her maiden voyage. Radiant in her fresh paint and dressed in flags, she also flew a long pennant that identified her as the new Blue Ribband champion. On that maiden crossing she broke the record of Italy's *Rex*. Among her fortunate and excited passengers was Mme. Lebrun, the first lady of France. And long after the ship was secured at Pier 88, which was built especially for her by the city government, that first round of guests and visitors and the press came back ashore in unanimous, ecstatic praise: she was the most spectacular liner of all time!

She was, of course, something of a giant step (and a big gamble) for the French; they had never built a ship of such mammoth proportions (the very first to exceed "at least 60,000 tons and 1,000 feet") and exceptional might (she had to be a Blue Ribband winner). By some measures, she was almost twice the size of their previous flagship, the *Ile de France*.

Record-breaking, prestigious, "the supreme symbol of all that is France," the *Normandie*, however, never fully realized the grand hopes she inspired. A financial disappointment, she rarely sailed at more than 60 percent of her capacity. Moreover, world affairs drastically abbreviated what should have been a long and glorious career. As Hitler's armies stormed into Poland in 1939, the *Normandie* was stranded in New York, never to sail again after only four years of commercial service. There she later burned and capsized, ending up on the scrap heap. When her last pieces were hauled ashore by wrecking crews, the magical *Normandie* was only twelve years old.

The *Normandie* was the ultimate ocean liner—at least of the thirties and perhaps of the century. Innovative, glittering, and exceptionally advanced, she was the culmination of a continuing series of lavishly designed and increasingly modern French Line passenger ships: the *France* of 1912, the *Paris* of 1921, the *Ile de France* of 1927, and the *Champlain* of 1932. Her designer, Vladimir Yourkevitch, took something from each of them and also from each of the other superliners of the world. He sought perfection and then some.

Her first keel plates were laid down in January 1931 at St.-Nazaire. In the ensuing months, evocative details of the new ship's statistics and accommodations were released with tantalizing frequency from the Paris home office, which was overwhelmed with suggestions for names: from *La Belle France* to *Président Paul Doumer*, the recently assassinated president of France. Even *Maurice Chevalier, Jean d'Arc,* and *General Pershing* were among the candidates. At the same time shipyard crews at Clydebank in Scotland had begun work on Britain's new national flagship and wonder liner. Something of a race had begun.

Madame Lebrun, the first lady of France, named the ship *Normandie* during the launch ceremonies (*left*) on October 29, 1932. The unfinished 28,000-ton hull slipped into the Loire with a backwash that swept a hundred workers and visitors into the water. Already she had a sense of the dramatic. [Built by Chantiers de l'Atlantique, St.-Nazaire, France, 1935. 82,799 gross tons; 1,028 feet long; 117 feet wide. Steam turboelectric engines, quadruple screw. Service speed 29 knots. 1,972 passengers (848 first class, 670 tourist class, 454 third class).]

The *Normandie*'s purpose was threefold: to be the world's largest liner (the first to exceed 1,000 feet in length and 60,000 tons), to be the fastest on the North Atlantic (although the French never publicly acknowledged this goal since, should she fail for some reason, the publicity damage could be ruinous), and to be a dazzling floating center of all that was France—art, decoration, technology. The government subsidized much of her construction cost.

But just as with the *Queen Mary*, construction work on the *Normandie* was temporarily stopped during the harshest Depression years. Her maiden voyage was postponed until the spring of 1935. She is shown at left while fitting out at St.-Nazaire on March 18, 1935.

Finally crossing in May 1935, she immediately captured the Blue Ribband with a record run of 29.98 knots, breaking the mark set by Italy's *Rex* of 28.92. The *Normandie* instantly became headline news. She is shown above on her visit to Southampton, being fed by no less than three tenders. The one in the center is the famous paddler *Lorna Doone*, which had previously been used as a sight-seeing craft.

Her New York arrival was tumultuous, perhaps the greatest that port had yet seen. Tugs, launches, fireboats, cutters, and pilot boats serenaded the record-breaking ship as she slowly made her way from Lower New York Bay to the north side of Pier 88, the terminal at West Forty-eighth Street that was barely complete for her first arrival.

The public marveled at the *Normandie*'s raked silhouette. In every way she was a ship of the future. Her three huge red-and-black funnels diminished in height moving aft, the third functioning as a dummy ventilator. Her outdoor upper decks were meticulously cleared: not a ventilator or deckhouse or chain locker out of place or even in sight. All these technical needs were cleverly hidden with great care below decks. The exquisitely raked bow was a masterful conjunction of form and function, contributing significantly to the vessel's record speed. But if her exterior appearance was striking, the interiors were the masterpiece.

The *Normandie* was certainly the most extravagantly decorated liner of her day, perhaps of all time. The main dining room (*above*) was done in hammered glass, bronze, and glistening Lalique towers of light. Slightly longer than the Hall of Mirrors at Versailles, it rose three decks high and seated a thousand guests. The theater was the first ever fitted to a liner and included a stage for live performances as well as movies. The indoor pool (*below*) was 80 feet of graduating levels. The Winter Garden (*opposite top*) included exotic birds in cages, sprays of water, and an abundance of plant life. The main lounge was covered in Dupas glass panels, and special Aubusson tapestries were used to upholster the chairs. The entrance to the grand salon (*opposite bottom*) had a huge urn of light as a centerpiece. Each adjoining first-class cabin was done in a distinctive decor, resulting in four hundred different themes overall. Two deluxe apartments headed this first-class section and were located on the sun deck, tucked away from all other accommodations. Each had a private terrace, four bedrooms, a living room, servants' quarters, and a dining room with private pantry. Visitors to the *Normandie* were almost always impressed with her elegance, her high quality, and her exceptional spaciousness.

Cie Gle Transatlantique . Paquebot « NORMANDIE » Un Coin du Fumoir

(photo Desboutin)

The *Normandie*'s first-class smoking room (*above*) and the ornate chapel (*below*).

Cie Gle Transatlantique . Paquebot « NORMANDIE » La Chapelle

(photo Desboutin)

The long gallery (*above*) and the grill room (*below*).

48   *The* Normandie   The promenade deck cabin-class foyer (*above*).

The great excitement of the *Normandie*'s debut was soon tempered by worries about the new Cunarder being built on the Clyde and due out within a year. An even greater concern, however, was the French flagship's bad bout of vibration during her maiden season on the Atlantic. Newly designed propellers eventually reduced this problem considerably. Another serious problem was the Blue Ribband. The *Normandie* held the prized title of world's fastest ship for little more than a year. Then, nearly three months after her own maiden crossing, the *Queen Mary* took the Ribband in August

1936 with a run of 30.14 knots. The *Normandie* regained the honors the following March, with a record of 30.9; that August she improved to 31.2. The rivalry ended in August 1938, when the *Queen Mary* proved the fastest, at 31.6 knots. Her record stood until surpassed in 1952 by the *United States*, with a record of over 36 knots.

The splendid views on this page and the next two pages were captured by the photographer Everett Viez on an eastbound passage on July 2, 1937. The uncluttered effect of the vast bow section (*below*) is clearly evident.

This aft view shows the tourist-class deck area and the novelty of the *Normandie*'s permanent outdoor pool on her northern run.

This is the tourist class aft deck section as seen looking forward from the third-class section. Note the barricades at the top of the stairwell.

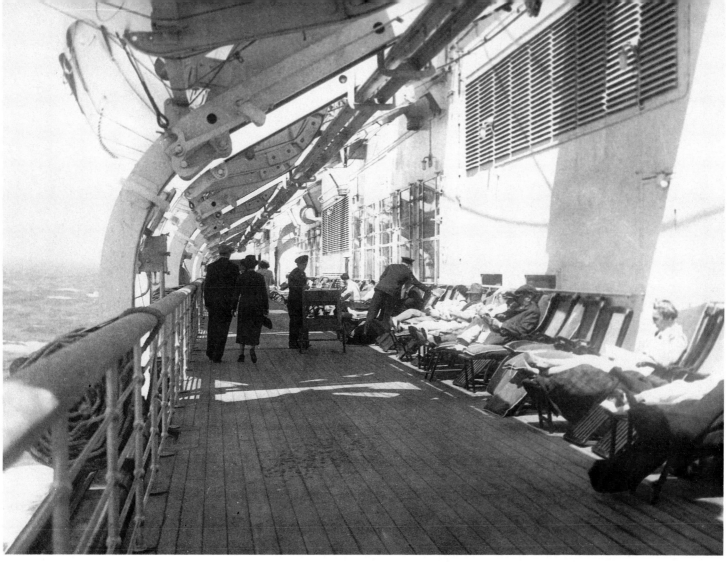

Tea is being served in this view looking forward on the port side of the boat deck. This was a first-class area.

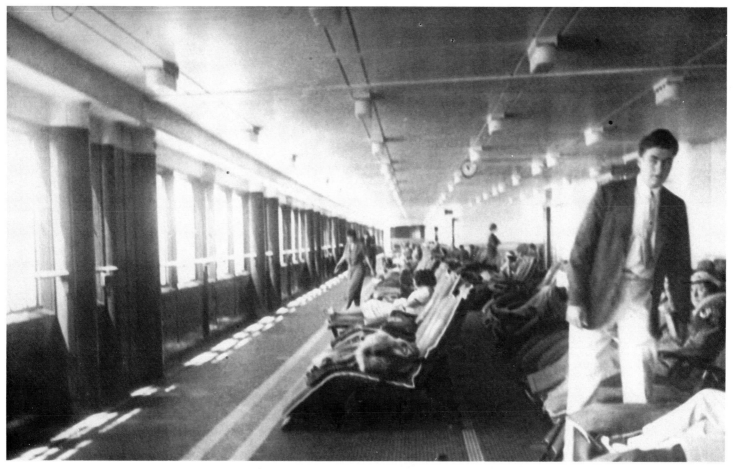

The view of the starboard enclosed promenade deck is seen facing aft.

The announcement came in the summer of 1935: at 80,000 tons the new *Queen Mary* would depose *Normandie* (a mere 79,280 tons) from her throne as the world's largest ship. Rising to the challenge, the French built a large deck house on one of the *Normandie*'s aft decks in her winter overhaul of 1935–36, just months before the Cunarder's first crossing; thus fattened, the *Normandie* tipped the scales at 83,423 tons, soundly surpassing the *Mary*'s 80,774 and retaining the heavyweight crown until the March 1940 arrival of the *Queen Elizabeth*, no mincing monarch at 83,673 tons—the new world champ.

In this aerial view (*above*) at Le Havre, the *Normandie* is being moved into that port's large graving dock to complete her 1935–36 winter overhaul. (The *Ile de France* can be seen at the left.) That aft deck house can also be seen in another aerial view (*left*) as she arrives off New York. In the third view (*opposite top*), dating from 1937, Meseck and Moran tugs assist in the docking of the French flagship, which is now sporting rebuilt, extended bridge wings.

One of the greatest gatherings of passenger ships along New York's Luxury Liner Row occurred on March 19, 1937 (*opposite bottom*).

From top to bottom: *Berengaria*, Cunard-White Star; the *Georgic*, also Cunard-White Star; the *Normandie*; the *Rex*, Italian Line; and the *Europa*, North German Lloyd.

On August 28, 1939, the *Normandie* was "temporarily" laid up at Pier 88 because of the imminence of war in Europe. She would never sail again. With the fall of France to the Nazis, keeping the giant ship in the safety of still-neutral U.S. waters seemed a sensible plan. The *Normandie* lay idle; her funnels were capped with canvas, her furnishings protected with dustcovers, and her staff reduced to a scant 115 for maintenance and security. She is shown above here on September 16, 1939, with (from left to right) the *Ile de France* (also laid up at the French Line pier), the *Queen Mary* (painted gray), the *Aquitania* (partially gray), and the *Rex*, still in "neutral" service to and from Mussolini's Italy.

There were rumors that the *Normandie* might become a troopship or even be rebuilt as an aircraft carrier. But it was not until December 12, 1941, five days after the attack on Pearl Harbor, that she was officially seized by the U.S. government. On December 27 she was transferred to the navy and was renamed the USS *Lafayette*. Her conversion into a massive, fifteen-thousand-capacity troopship began at pier side, using work crews from a local shipyard. Those luxurious fittings and artworks had to be removed and taken ashore. An incredible sense of urgency prevailed over the project. Soon after completion, in mid-February, she was slated to go to Boston for drydock and final outfitting as the war's second largest troopship.

On February 9 sparks from a workman's acetylene torch ignited a pile of kapok life jackets. The *Normandie* began to burn on that cold afternoon (*left*). Workers evacuated the ship, and soon fire-fighting units both ashore and afloat arrived at the scene. Midtown Manhattan was covered by a huge cloud of brownish smoke (*opposite top*). Anxiety engendered misjudgment: while the fire was very damaging, the fire fighters poured far too much water onto the smoldering liner. Early the next day she capsized at her berth and was soon declared a complete loss. The first aerial view of the capsized *Normandie*, taken on February 10, 1941 (*opposite bottom*).

On her side the 1,028-foot long former *Normandie* presented the most difficult salvage job yet. Her funnels, her masts, and finally all of her upper superstructure had to be systematically removed by floating cranes that used nearby barges. Simultaneously, great pumps pushed Hudson River water out of her vast, burned-out hulk. This exceptional operation was finally completed some fifteen months later, in the summer of 1943. Rumors resurfaced that she would be rebuilt as an aircraft carrier.

In November 1943 the *Normandie* (shown below off Lower Manhattan) was towed to a Bayonne, New Jersey, graving dock for inspection and then to a Brooklyn pier for lay-up. No decision was made on her future. Two years later, in October 1945, she was stricken from the navy's list of ships and was offered for disposal. Her original designer suggested cutting her down in size, to about 30,000 tons, and rebuilding her as a passenger ship. But nothing came to pass. The U.S. government had no interest, and so in October 1946 she was sold to a New Jersey scrapping company. Within twelve months her long hull was gone.

5. REFIT, RESTORATION, REVIVAL

World War II devastated the French Line. That grand fleet of the thirties was a shambles, mostly destroyed. The *Lafayette* and the *Paris* had been lost just before the war started. The *Champlain* was sunk soon after France fell. And worst of all, the splendid *Normandie* had burned while docked in New York and was later scrapped by the Americans. Even the smallish *De Grasse* was nearly a complete loss. She was sunk in the summer of 1944 but then was salvaged exactly a year later.

As though fitting the pieces of a complex puzzle, the CGT's Paris offices began, in that first summer of peace in 1945, to reassemble their passenger fleet. Heroic and proud, the *Ile de France* was the largest survivor (but, in fact, she would not be fully restored until as late as 1949). Then there was the *Colombie*, which, like the *Ile*, had been in Allied hands. But she, too, needed extensive work, perhaps for two years or more. The St.-Nazaire yard was still suffering from shortages of both manpower and materials in those first months of liberation. Their efforts were sluggish at best. In fact, American equipment and supplies were rushed over to St.-Nazaire and to the heavily bombed port of Le Havre.

The actual resumption of the CGT's transatlantic service was provisional at best. In May 1945, just weeks after VE Day, the 7,706-ton passenger-freighter *Oregon* left New York for Le Havre. Originally built in 1929 to sail from Le Havre to the North American Pacific coast via Panama, she had quarters for only thirty-eight first-class passengers but expanded to seventy-six by doubling the number of occupants in each cabin. When she sailed again, in late June, she was described as "the first passenger ship whose departure from New York has been made public since the USA entered the war in December 1941." A sister ship, the *Wisconsin*, made similar sailings well into 1946.

Three wartime passenger ships from Messageries Maritimes—the *Maréchal Joffre*, the *Indochinois*, and the *Athos II*—also assisted on the New York run. And when the *Ile de France* was handed back by the British in February 1946, she began a series of austerity sailings between Southampton, Cherbourg (Le Havre was still too heavily damaged), Halifax, and Boston. Later, when sailing from Cherbourg to New York in October 1946, she carried 1,689 passengers plus returning troops. Even her priority passengers had to share staterooms with six or seven others. She was finally released in the spring of 1947 and then steamed for St.-Nazaire and long-overdue repairs, reconstruction, and refitting. Among the many changes the CGT designers made was modernizing her by eliminating one of her original three stacks.

The *Colombie* also made a few austerity New York sailings, including one with hundreds of French seamen who were going to the States to take delivery of the nineteen Liberty Ships being given to the French Line as reparations and aid. It was finally left to the *De Grasse* to reopen formal commercial service. She had two years at St.-Nazaire before reopening Le Havre–New York sailings in July 1947. With a greatly reduced capacity of 720 passengers in two classes and sporting a new single funnel, she maintained the French Line alone for two years. What an exceptional contrast to those lustrous years before the war, when the *De Grasse* sailed in company with the *Normandie*, the *Ile de France*, the *Paris*, the *Champlain*, and the *Lafayette*.

OREGON

Immediately after the war in Europe ended in May 1945, the combination passenger-cargo ship *Oregon* (*above*) reopened the French Line passenger run between Le Havre and New York. Originally built to carry thirty-eight first-class passengers only, she was reconfigured to accommodate seventy-six. She continued on the New York service until October 1948 and was teamed with another combination ship, the *Wisconsin*.

The *Oregon* was completed in October 1929 for the Le Havre–Baltimore service. Later she was assigned to the North American West Coast run, sailing from Le Havre to Puerto Colombia, the Panama Canal, La Libertad, San José, Los Angeles, San Francisco, and Vancouver. Used by the Allies during the war, she went on the Le Havre–Central America service in 1948 before being leased to Messageries Maritimes for five years, from 1950 until 1955. She finished her days as the Panamanian-flag *Pacific Harmony* before going to Far Eastern breakers. [Built by Bremer-Vulkan Shipyards, Bremen, Germany, 1929. 7,706 gross tons; 473 feet long; 61 feet wide. MAN-type diesels, twin screw. Service speed 13 knots. 76 first-class passengers.]

DE GRASSE

After a two-year refit (1945–47) at St.-Nazaire, the *De Grasse* (*below*) was the first liner to restore the French Line's commercial service between Le Havre and New York. She received a gala welcome when she arrived at New York on July 25, 1947. She had been modernized and her quarters made more spacious, with berths for 500 in cabin class and 470 in tourist class. But most noticeably, her original twin thin funnels were gone, replaced by one with a rakish slope. Fully booked on that second maiden voyage, she also carried cargo, including the large bulletproof Mercedes that had once belonged to Adolf Hitler. Now owned by the French government, it was bound for an exhibition in Toronto.

Berths on the *De Grasse*'s first two seasons were booked well in advance. She ran single-handedly throughout the year. The return of a restored *Ile de France*, at first slated for 1948, was delayed and finally rescheduled for the summer of 1949. The completion of the *Liberté*, the former *Europa*, seemed even more remote. She was not due until the mid-1950s. In 1952, after the arrival of the new *Flandre*, the *De Grasse*, by then nearly thirty years old, was moved permanently to the Le Havre–West Indies run in company with another prewar ship, the *Colombie* of 1931. The *De Grasse*, soon to be replaced by the brand new *Antilles*, was expected to go to the scrappers, but in the winter of 1953, Canadian Pacific Steamships was in rather desperate need of a passenger ship: it was coronation year, traffic would be especially heavy, and the company's *Empress of Canada* had just been lost in a Liverpool pierside fire. The *De Grasse* was the perfect temporary replacement. That spring she hoisted the British colors, became the *Empress of Australia*, and began sailing on the Liverpool-Montreal run.

Sold in early 1956 to the Italians, to the Grimaldi-Siosa Lines, the *Empress of Australia* became the migrant ship *Venezuela*. She sailed between Italy and the Caribbean. She stranded on the rocks near Cannes on March 17, 1962, and became a complete loss. That summer she was towed to La Spezia, Italy, and broken up.

COLOMBIE

The *Colombie* was seized by the Americans at Casablanca just after the attack on Pearl Harbor in December 1941. She was later converted into a troopship with a capacity of 2,683, a dramatic increase over her 491 prewar passenger berths. Mostly used on the North Atlantic run, she was placed under a partnered operation of the American War Shipping Administration and the exiled French Line offices in New York. In 1945 the demand for hospital ships was quite staggering; the *Colombie* was sent to a Brooklyn shipyard and refitted to carry 828 patients just in time for VE Day. She was renamed the USS *Aleda E. Lutz* in honor of a U.S. Army lieutenant killed in a plane crash over southern France in November 1944 after having participated in 190 missions to rescue wounded personnel. After spending considerable time in Pacific waters, the ship was officially returned to the French Line at Pier 88 in New York on April 11, 1946 (*left*).

The *Colombie* made several austerity sailings for the French Line in 1946 and was then leased to the French government for further trooping out to troubled colonial Indochina. Two years later she was sent to the de Schelde shipyard at Flushing in the Netherlands for a twenty-four-month overhaul and modernization. Her original twin stacks were replaced by a single tapered funnel (*left*). Her passenger quarters were upgraded and the configuration modified to 192 in first class, 140 in cabin class, and 246 in tourist class. She resumed her West Indies sailings from Le Havre and Southampton in November 1950. Previously, her place had been taken by the chartered Greek Line passenger ship *Katoomba*, a ship dating from 1913 and one of the last coal burners on the Atlantic. Partnered with the new *Antilles* after 1953, the *Colombie* also ran occasional cruises from Le Havre.

The thirty-three-year-old ship was sold to Greek buyers, the Typaldos Lines, in 1964 and renamed *Atlantica* for Mediterranean cruising, mostly out of Venice. But when that company closed in 1966–67, the aged ship was laid up near Piraeus. While there were reports that she was scrapped in 1970, she was, in fact, only partially dismantled. Four years later, in May 1974, her hull was towed to Barcelona for final scrapping.

ILE DE FRANCE

The largest liner left in the French fleet, the *Ile de France* was officially decommissioned by the British in September 1945. She is shown above at that time while being handed over and undergoing repairs at the Todd Shipyards in Hoboken, New Jersey. A 7,500-ton Victory Ship stands alongside, about to enter the dry dock. But there was little time for a full refit for the *Ile*. She was hurriedly sent off on further trooping, repatria-tion, and austerity voyages to Canada, New York, and even far-off Indochina.

In the spring of 1947, the hardworking *Ile de France* was handed back to the French Line and then was sent to St.-Nazaire for rebuilding. The task took more than two years. Her third dummy funnel came off in one of the most thorough conversions of any major postwar liner (shown below at St.-Nazaire).

A pair of new, more streamlined stacks were added. Her modernized interiors included a more contemporary berthing pattern of 541 in first class, 577 in cabin class, and 227 in tourist class. In the view above, from June 1949, she is taking a last turn at the fitting-out dock at St.-Nazaire before reentering French Line service in July. Note the *Liberté* in the background, still a year away from the completion of her own postwar transformation.

The *Ile de France* left Le Havre on July 25, 1949, on her postwar crossing to New York. That night she called at Southampton's Ocean Dock (*below*) to take on additional passengers. It was her first call there as a luxury liner since September 3, 1939, just a few hours after war was officially declared. She called at Southampton in 1945–47 as a troopship. Relisted at 44,356 gross tons, the *Ile* ranked at this time as the fourth-largest liner afloat, following the *Queen Elizabeth*, the *Queen Mary*, and the still refitting *Liberté*.

Also at the Ocean Dock is the British troopship *Eastern Prince*, used in prewar South American service for the Furness Prince Line.

When she returned to New York in August 1949, the *Ile de France* received a festive welcome that included tugs, fireboats, and a U.S. Navy blimp overhead (*above*). Her return came as a great relief to the 17,000-ton *De Grasse*, which for two years had been sailing single-handedly for the French. Both ships were joined in August 1950 by the 51,000-ton *Liberté*, totally restored as the national flagship.

Here is a sample schedule for the three ships from New York in 1951:

Ile de France	Saturday, May 5	Noon
Liberté	Saturday, May 12	Noon
De Grasse	Tuesday, May 22	11:00 A.M.
Ile de France	Wednesday, May 23	4:00 P.M.
Liberté	Tuesday, May 29	11:00 P.M.

When the *Ile de France* was restored in the late forties, warehouses were thoroughly inventoried for furniture, including pieces from the *Normandie*. Many items found their way onto the *Ile* and later onto the *Liberté*. Both ships were decorated in contemporary styles that reflected the luxurious art deco themes for which the French liners had been noted in the prewar years. The Café de Paris (*left*) on board the *Ile* was decorated by Le Bucheron and featured a transparent dance floor that was lighted from below in various colors. The room was a combination smoking room, bar, lounge, and cabaret setting for first-class passengers and was located aft on the promenade deck. A mahogany bar at one end matched the mahogany of the walls and the brown color of the furniture.

The same chairs were brought out of storage for the first-class restaurant (*right*), but crystal lighting fixtures and the wall coverings were among the changes made by 1949. The grand stairwell remained. For private entertaining, two small dining rooms were located just forward. Expectedly, the cooking remained impeccable. That 1930s French Line publicity slogan remained true: "More seagulls followed the French liners than any other because the scraps were better!"

The *Ile de France* featured a sumptuous array of first-class suites and deluxe staterooms. The Chantilly Suite (*top left*), for example, was especially designed by Leleu and was done in slightly glazed, veneered sycamore. It included a sitting room, bedroom, trunk room, and full bathroom. The sitting room, which had the "dead leaf" pattern to the sycamore, was dominated by decorative panels depicting the castle at Chantilly.

The cabin-class drawing room (*top right*) was connected to the smoking room above by an illuminated glass stairwell. Decorated by Le Bucheron, it was enhanced by the great bay windows that overlooked the forward part of the ship.

With thundering whistles sounding her departure, the *Ile de France* prepares for another departure from New York's Pier 88 (*bottom left*). She would cross to Plymouth in six days and Le Havre in seven. The French Line prided itself on its renowned seamanship and hotel skills. One of her masters, Captain Cailloce, poses on the starboard bridge of the *Ile* while at sea (*bottom right*).

On another occasion three bedroom stewardesses (*above*) pose on the top deck of the *Ile de France* during one of its stays in New York. Like all great steamship lines, the French Line had employees, both ashore and afloat, who followed forebears and remained with the line for decades and others, such as deckhands and waiters, who joined only for a summer season of travel.

Just as the likes of Noel Coward, Olivia de Havilland, Fred Astaire, Walt Disney, and the Grand Duchess Marie of Russia had crossed on French liners in the twenties and thirties, so a steady flow of celebrities crossed on the *Ile de France* and the *Liberté* in the fifties. Alan Ladd and family appear below. Other celebrated voyagers appear on the next page.

Jane Powell

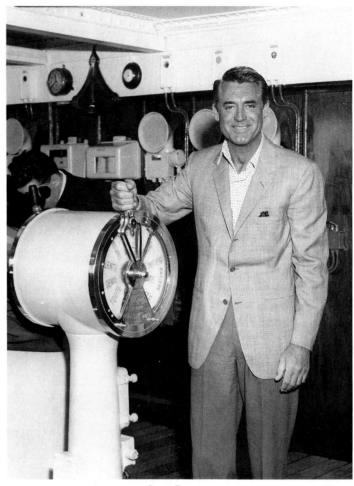

Cary Grant

Kim Novak

Maurice Chevalier

The *Ile de France* made headline news on several occasions in the later years of her career. In July 1956, while outbound from New York, she rescued 753 survivors from the sinking Italian liner *Andrea Doria*. Shown returning to New York, she was later given a special plaque by the U.S. Coast Guard citing her for her gallant efforts. Today it is in the French Line collection at Le Havre.

In October 1956 she was lashed by a violent North Atlantic storm. Six passenger cabins were flooded, and her superstructure was dented. In February 1957, during one of her winter Caribbean cruises (here she is shown departing on an earlier cruise on an ice-filled Hudson on January 6, 1956), she went aground at Fort-de-France on Martinique. The damage was considerable. Her passengers were forced ashore and later had to be flown home. An oceangoing tug was summoned and later towed the liner to the Newport News Shipyards in Virginia, the nearest facility capable of handling her in drydock and making the necessary repairs.

The *Ile de France* turned thirty-one in 1958, the same year that the first jets flew the North Atlantic. Understandably, her passenger loads were diminishing, and the problems of old age were setting in. There were bursting pipes, engine malfunctions, and ever-increasing fuel oil costs for her hoary turbine machinery. That November she sailed from New York for the last time (shown). Her fate sparked many rumors. Some wanted her for a museum, another for a hotel along the Riviera, and the Sheraton Corporation for a tourist and convention center off Martinique. Another plan, wildly ambitious, suggested that her masts and funnels be temporarily cut down for bridge clearance so that she could be sailed along the Seine into the heart of Paris. In the end Japanese scrappers offered the highest bid.

Le Havre was crowded with tearful well-wishers when the ship departed for Osaka on February 26, 1959. Under the command of a small Japanese crew, she hoisted the Japanese flag at sea and became the *Furansu Maru* (*France Maru*). But then, much to the horror of the Paris headquarters, the scrappers chartered her for $4,000 a day to MGM studios for use as a floating prop in the disaster film *The Last Voyage*. Dubbed the *Claridon*, a fictional transpacific liner, she was moored in the Inland Sea as the forward funnel was released deliberately and sent crashing down, the watertight compartments partly flooded, and those elegant interiors peppered with small explosions. Later, she was brought into Osaka and reduced to rubble. Her overall impact and style were considerable, and her place in twentieth-century ocean-liner history is assured.

6. GLORIOUS PRIZE OF WAR: THE LIBERTÉ

The grand fleet of great Atlantic superliners of the thirties was cut by more than half by the war's end in 1945. The *Normandie*, the *Bremen*, the *Empress of Britain*, the *Rex*, and the *Conte di Savoia* were gone. The aged *Aquitania* would never see commercial service again. The three largest liners left were the *Queen Elizabeth*, the *Queen Mary*, and the very neglected, very rusted *Europa*.

That prewar German record breaker (she held the Blue Ribband from 1930 to 1933) had been lying at Bremerhaven since the late summer of 1939. She was to have been converted into a large landing ship for the planned Nazi invasion of Britain and later as an aircraft carrier, but neither change ever came to pass. So in May 1945 American invasion forces arriving in Bremen found what was by then the third-largest liner afloat. Soon claimed by the Americans, she became, after some hurried repairs, the troopship USS *Europa*. But after a few trips across the North Atlantic with mostly GI passengers, she was found to have serious problems. The constant outbreak of small fires was one of them. The U.S. government soon lost interest and donated her to the French, who needed suitable reparation for the loss of the *Normandie* four years earlier. Appropriately renamed *Liberté*, she became one of the French Line's most popular and successful ships.

The French Line's *Liberté* was the reincarnation of one of the great prewar Atlantic superliners, North German Lloyd's *Europa*, which had captured the Blue Ribband with a record run of 27.91 knots. She and her near sister, the *Bremen*, were the pride of the German merchant fleet. Later in the thirties, thought was given to reengining this pair to outpace both the *Normandie* and the *Queen Mary*, the next record breakers. However, nothing ever went beyond the planning stage. The *Bremen* was lost to a fire at her Bremerhaven berth in March 1941, but the *Europa* somehow survived the war intact.

She was a very neglected, rusty ship when U.S. forces reached Bremerhaven soon after the collapse of the Nazi regime in May 1945. She had even survived last-minute orders from the Nazi high command to sink her at her pier. Inside the ship the American invasion forces found signs of some troop provision for voyages she never made. She was soon designated AP-177, the USS *Europa*.

She was given some temporary repairs and was later dry-docked at New York (at Bayonne and then at Hoboken, where she is shown in this view) before commencing regular American troopship service that September. Her capacity was officially listed at 4,300, with 900 crew. However, she was soon plagued by small fires caused, it was determined, by the removal of her original high-quality fittings and their replacement with inferior items by the Germans, who were desperate for materials during the war. Furthermore, some serious hull cracks were uncovered, which prompted safety concerns among U.S. Coast Guard authorities. The USS *Europa*'s spell of service as an American troopship was shortived. In early 1946 she was handed over to the International Reparations Commission. [Built by Blohm & Voss Shipbuilders, Hamburg, Germany, 1930. 49,746 gross tons; 936 feet long; 102 feet wide. Steam turbines, quadruple screw. Service speed 27 knots. 2,024 passengers as built (687 first class, 524 second class, 306 tourist class, 507 third class).]

Having lost the *Normandie*, the French were in dire need of a large passenger liner. They were anxious to reestablish something of their luxurious passenger service, and, it was thought, with proper modifications the *Europa* could be made to appear French. Consequently, she crossed to Le Havre and first had her funnels repainted in French Line red and black. After considering the name *Lorraine*, officials settled on the more appropriate *Liberté*.

Then misfortune struck on December 8, 1946: as the idle *Liberté* was pulled from her moorings by a fierce Atlantic gale, she slammed into the sunken wreckage of the liner *Paris*. The larger ship soon settled in Le Havre harbor (*above*). She had a large gash in her hull but fortunately remained upright. Refit work ceased as salvage took priority.

She was refloated by the following spring, on April 15, and then was towed to St.-Nazaire. Her $19-million restoration program began. She was to be changed from Teutonic record breaker to French luxury flagship. But there were more tense moments when, in October 1949, a fire at St.-Nazaire damaged her freshly restored interiors and caused further delay.

The fresh black paint on the *Liberté*'s hull has peeled without benefit of an undercoat (*opposite bottom*), which is typical of a maiden crossing. She is in the mid-Atlantic steaming westbound, as viewed from the top deck of the eastbound *Ile de France*. She arrived to a fireboat and tug reception at New York on August 17, 1950, as the new flagship of the French Line. She was paired with the *Ile de France* and the smaller *De Grasse*. Since her tonnage had increased to 51,839, she was for a time listed as the world's third-largest liner, following the *Queen Elizabeth* and the *Queen Mary*. In the summer of 1952, following the arrival of the record-breaking *United States*, she dropped to fourth place. In the aerial view above, as the *Liberté* approaches Pier 88 three other Atlantic liners are in port: the *Conte Biancamano* of the Italian Line, the *Caronia* of Cunard (only her large single funnel is actually visible), and, at the far left, the *Gripsholm* of the Swedish-American Line.

Outbound from New York City on August 25, 1950, on the return leg of her maiden voyage, the *Liberté* passed the inbound *Ile de France* just off West Thirtieth Street in Manhattan. It was a joyous occasion for the French, who now had two large luxury liners on the North Atlantic run.

After her postwar refit, the *Liberté* accommodated 569 in first class, 562 in cabin class, and 382 in tourist class. Peak summer-season fares in 1950–51 were listed at $340 for first class, $230 for cabin class, and $170 for tourist class. Port taxes were levied only at Le Havre and ranged from $2 to $6, depending on class.

Internally, the *Liberté* was a splendid ship, in keeping with the fine decorative traditions of the French Line. Indeed, she had lost almost all of her German character and now was a true representative of France.

The first-class dining room (*top*) retained an impressive 1930s quality, while the library (*middle*) had a more luxurious tone. The theater (*bottom*) was one of the largest on the Atlantic in the fifties, with a capacity of 444.

To improve smoke deflection, the *Liberté*'s funnels were fitted with domed tops during her annual winter overhaul at St.-Nazaire in 1953–54.

Along with the *United States*, she could boast of the mightiest funnels then afloat.

As was customary for transatlantic liners in the fifties, the *Liberté* continued her Northern relays even in the dead of winter. Occasionally she was delayed by ferocious storms. At least once, at New York, she was behind schedule and arrived early one morning and then sailed by midnight the same day. In the view above, with the liner's black hull cloaked in ice and with the Hudson River seemingly frozen over, a Moran tug assists the *Liberté* on a midday departure in 1955.

A dramatic view (*left*) of the *Liberté* at Le Havre as she takes on her high-grade cargo, which often included the latest Paris fashions bound for the showrooms and shops of New York. She would often remain at Le Havre and at New York for two to four days between crossings.

In the aerial view above, dating from December 6, 1957, the *Liberté* is among the nine passenger liners berthed along New York's Luxury Liner Row. Shown from top to bottom, there are the *Berlin*, North German Lloyd; the *Ocean Monarch*, Furness–Bermuda Line; the *Parthia* and the *Queen Elizabeth*, Cunard Line; the *Liberté*; the *United States* and the *America*, United States Lines; the *Augustus*, Italian Line; and finally the *Independence*, American Export Lines.

When the 66,000-ton *France* was ordered in 1956, it was realized that the *Ile de France* and then the *Liberté* would be retired. The *Ile* was withdrawn in the fall of 1958, and the *Liberté* followed three years later, in November 1961. She left New York in a special farewell, one of the few liners accorded a fireboat and tug send-off (*below*). At Le Havre, she was berthed briefly in company with her successor, which was then preparing for her maiden voyage.

At first there were rumors that the *Liberté* would become a floating hotel at Seattle for the World's Fair there in 1962. But this did not materialize. Instead, she was sold to Italian ship breakers at La Spezia, where she arrived on January 30, 1962. Stripped of her lifeboats and with her aft decks and mast already gone, the *Liberté* was dismantled from the stern section forward. By June the demolition was complete.

7. SMART NEW SISTERS: THE FLANDRE AND THE ANTILLES

Its fleet badly depleted by the war, the French Line's directors eventually began to think of building new passenger ships. But their thinking was quite conservative, restrained even. There was the matter of finances, but in the hazy distance loomed another factor: the airplane. Furthermore, the French already had two big liners—the restored *Ile de France* and the transformed *Liberté*—to rival the likes of the two Cunard *Queens*, the *Mauretania*, the *America*, and the *Nieuw Amsterdam*. Only one brand-new superliner was being readied then, the speedy *United States*. The two French liners were assisted on the New York run by a third ship, the smallish and aging *De Grasse*. A third ship was still needed to create a weekly sailing in each direction, especially in the peak summer season.

When the designs for a pair of 20,000-tonners were completed, however, they were for the Le Havre–West Indies trade instead. One of them replaced the prewar *Colombie*, which had been working single-handedly in the early fifties. Similarly, at the same time, the Italian Line's first postwar liners, the *Augustus* and the *Giulio Cesare*, were used for the Italy–South America run rather than the seemingly more important New York trade. But as the first of these new French liners, the *Flandre*, was nearing completion, there was a change of plans. She would go on the New York service, at least for half of the year, while the veteran *De Grasse* would be retired. The second new ship, the *Antilles*, would join the *Colombie* in full-time Caribbean duties. Plans to retire the latter ship had been changed as well.

Like the French Line cabin steamers of the past, these were moderate, sensible, modern-looking ships with tapered stacks, a mast above the wheel-house area, raked bows, and electric cranes instead of the traditional booms and king posts. The *Flandre*, which later changed hands several times, wore a black hull for her northern sailings; the *Antilles* used tropical all-white. Both became well-known, favored ships. But in the end both ships had endings common to French Line and French-built passenger ships: fires. In fact, as recently as 1995 the last scarred and mangled remains of the fire-gutted *Flandre* were being cut up by ship breakers in Turkey.

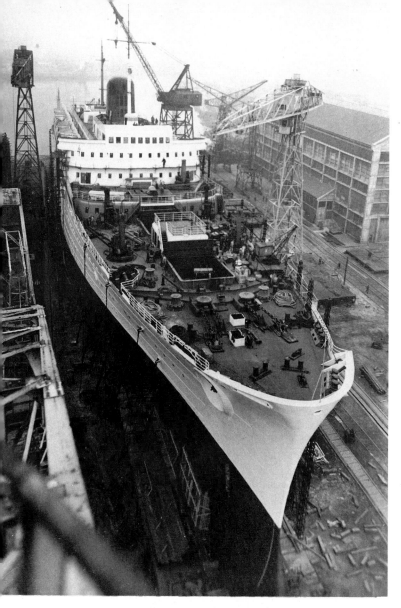

FLANDRE (1952)

This smart-looking passenger ship, the brand-new major liner for the French Line following World War II, was intended for the Le Havre–West Indies service even as she was being fitted out at her Dunkirk birthplace (as shown). But then there was some rethinking, and, with her hull repainted in black, she was reassigned to the Le Havre–New York run, at least for most of the year. She had troubles at the start of her long and varied career. She broke down on her maiden voyage in July 1952. Temporarily repaired, she finally reached Lower New York Bay (where she is shown below with a Moran tugboat alongside) but then broke down again. She couldn't even raise her own anchors or blast her whistle. Anticipated with great excitement, her maiden arrival was a dismal, embarrassing flop. Dressed in celebratory flags and greeted by whistles from other ships along the route, she had to be towed to her Pier 88 berth. Unsympathetic, Manhattan dockers thereafter referred to her as the "Flounder." [Built by Ateliers et Chantiers de France, Dunkirk, France, 1952. 20,469 gross tons; 600 feet long; 80 feet wide. Steam turbines, twin screw. Service speed 22 knots. 784 passengers (402 first class, 285 cabin class, 97 tourist class).]

The *Flandre*'s first-class section was air-conditioned in all public rooms and in about 90 percent of the cabins (the exceptions being a few on the forward end of the main deck). Most of these rooms were outside, and many had private bathrooms. The main salon was convertible to a theater, and there were glass-enclosed verandas along both sides of the ship. As in the prewar *Champlain*, the smoking room (*top left*) was decorated in a playing-card motif and included an illuminated dance floor. It opened onto the Lido Deck, which included an outdoor pool (*top right*) and adjacent open-air bar.

In tourist class on the *Flandre*, only the public rooms were air-conditioned. The cabins, such as this outside four-berth room (*bottom right*), lacked private bathrooms. The public rooms—which included the main salon, winter garden, reading-writing room, and the dining room on A deck—emphasized light and spaciousness with such woods as teak, ash, and birch.

September 3, 1957, was not merely the day after Labor Day, but a "labor day" along New York's waterfront. Within ten hours no fewer than twelve passenger liners, including the *Flandre*, debarked 9,386 passengers. It was 1,100 more than the one-day high set by nine liners in 1950. Seven liners are seen above in this aerial view (from left to right): the *Britannic*, the *Queen Mary*, and the *Mauretania* of Cunard; the *Flandre*; the *Olympia* of the Greek Line; the *United States* of United States Lines; and the *Independence* of American Export Lines.

First partnered with the *Ile de France* and the *Liberté*, the smallish *Flandre* spent one season, 1962, sailing alongside the sumptuous new *France*. Afterward she joined her sister, the *Antilles*, in full-time Caribbean service. This later run included some winter air-sea cruises out of Fort-de-France that were marketed to North American travelers. She joined Italy's Costa Line in 1968 and was rebuilt as an all-first-class cruise ship, the *Carla C*. However, after completion of an extensive refit, she went directly on charter to Princess Cruises, then a new West Coast firm, and was marketed as their *Princess Carla* (she was never officially renamed). Some of the first scripts for the *Love Boat* television series were written aboard her during cruises to Mexico and through the Panama Canal to the Caribbean. Costa later recalled the ship for its own lower Caribbean cruise service out of San Juan. She underwent major surgery at an Amsterdam shipyard in 1974, when her original steam turbines were replaced by new Dutch diesels. Later renamed *Carla Costa*, she was sold to Greece's Epirotiki Lines in 1992.

In her Greek incarnation she ran mainly seven-day cruises from Piraeus (Athens) to the Aegean isles and Turkey as the *Pallas Athena*. She was destroyed by fire on March 23, 1994. She had just disembarked her last cruise passenger at Piraeus when the fire started in an empty passenger cabin and then spread quickly. Badly scarred and with her upper decks collapsing within, she was towed to the outer harbor (shown in July 1994) and officially declared a complete wreck. Later that year, on Christmas Day, she arrived under tow at nearby Aliaga, Turkey, for demolition.

ANTILLES

Commissioned in January 1953, the *Antilles* (*below*) was a near sister to the *Flandre* and fortunately suffered none of that other ship's woes on her first sailing. First used for some "show-off" cruises to the Atlantic isles and the Mediterranean, the *Antilles* crossed to the Caribbean for the first time the following May. While her overall routing often varied, she normally sailed between Le Havre and Southampton to Vigo, San Juan, Pointe-à-Pitre, Fort-de-France, La Guaira, Trinidad, and Barbados. Periodically, she was sent on more extended voyages, which included calls at such ports as New Orleans, Galveston, Bermuda, Nassau, Kingston, Grand Cayman, and Veracruz. First teamed with the prewar *Colombie* and then (after 1962) with the *Flandre*, she began sailing alone after 1967.

The *Antilles* was destroyed by fire on January 8, 1971. While homeward bound from San Juan to Le Havre, she struck an uncharted reef off the tiny island of Mustique. Leaking fuel oil erupted into a fire, which rapidly spread throughout the ship. Her 635 passengers and crew were evacuated and were later rescued by Cunard's *Queen Elizabeth 2* and two nearby French Line freighters. A day later the fire-ravaged *Antilles* began to sink. On January 18, she broke in half and still later broke into three pieces. For many years thereafter, she was stranded on that same reef off Mustique, her rust-colored bow pointed downward, her funnel and upperworks collapsed within, and the stern section canting aft. Since scrapping would have been extremely difficult and expensive, she remained something of a Caribbean ruin until the late 1980s. The remains broke up and fell into the sea. [Built by the Naval Dockyard, Brest, France, 1952. 19,828 gross tons; 599 feet long; 80 feet wide. Steam turbines, twin screw. Service speed 22 knots. 778 passengers (404 first class, 285 cabin class, 89 tourist class).]

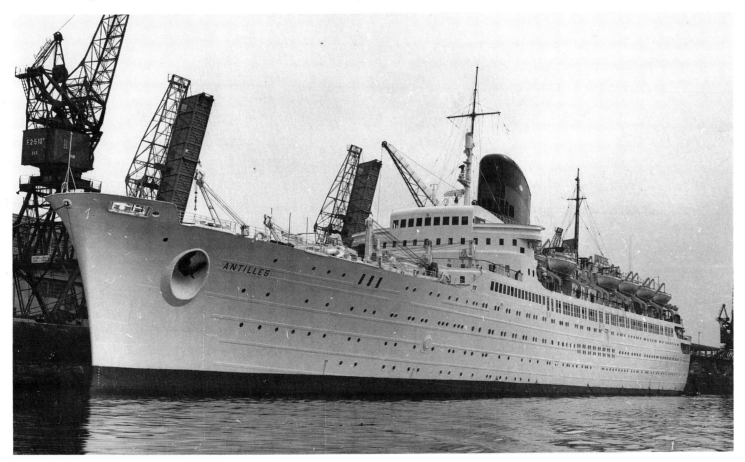

DE GRASSE (1956)

After the loss of the *Antilles*, the French Line was in rather desperate need of an adequate replacement liner. Although listed on the Norwegian America Line schedules for two more years, the fifteen-year-old *Bergensfjord* was sold for a sum greater than her Oslo-based owners could refuse. She was transferred to the French in March 1971 and was renamed *De Grasse* (*Louisiane* had been the initial choice). Almost immediately she entered a French shipyard for a six-month refit and refurbishing that included the creation of all-first-class accommodations for 581 passengers. Unfortunately, soon after entering the Le Havre–Southampton–West Indies service that November, she met with only slight success. Rather quickly, the old trade demands had fallen away, siphoned off by the airlines. The French sought an alternative, however, by using her for West Indies cruises out of San Juan. Furthermore, there were trips in European waters: from Le Havre to Norway and the Baltic, and from Cannes to the Mediterranean, the Black Sea, and West Africa. Unhappily, none of these proved a financial success. In the fall of 1973, she was placed on the sales lists.

Although rumored to become an Israeli hotel and casino ship, she was sold to Norwegian interests, placed under the Singapore flag, and renamed *Rasa Sayang* (Flower of the East) for Pacific Ocean cruising. She became quite popular until, she caught fire at sea on June 6, 1977, and was adrift for some time. She was repaired, but publicity about the fire in the travel press ruined her reputation. She was laid up in June 1978 and later sold to Greek buyers, who renamed her *Golden Moon*, intending to use her in the Mediterranean. A year later she was reportedly being chartered to a Dutch travel firm for use as the *Prins Van Oranje*. But neither project came to pass. Finally the London-based CTC Lines leased her for cruises out of Sydney, Australia, under her earlier name of *Rasa Sayang*. But on August 27, 1980, while undergoing repairs near Piraeus, Greece, she was swept by fire. Her charred hull had to be towed to nearby Kynosoura and then deliberately sunk. [Built by Swan, Hunter & Wigham Richardson Limited, Wallsend-on-Tyne, England, 1956. 18,739 gross tons; 578 feet long; 72 feet wide. Stork diesels, twin screw. Service speed 20 knots. 581 all-first-class passengers.]

8. OTHER FRENCHMEN

The yellowed pages of a copy of the *Official Steamship and Airways Guide*, a monthly bible of the travel industry from the fifties, list about a dozen different French passenger lines. They spanned the globe. In the far corners and back rooms of the French Line's offices in New York, one just above Battery Park in lower Manhattan and the other, appropriately, in the Maison Française at Rockefeller Center, there were racks of brochures, sailing schedules, and rate sheets on these firms and on their less familiar ships.

Messageries Maritimes was still the second largest under the tricolor. They had an almost new fleet, mostly of combination passenger-cargo liners built after the war, in the early fifties. They all sailed from Marseilles, offering connections from Le Havre via Paris. There were the "three musketeers"—the *Cambodge*, the *Laos*, and the *Viet-Nam*—to the Far East; the sisters *Calédonien* and *Tahitien* to the South Pacific and Australia; and the four sisters of the *La Bourdonnais* class to Mauritius.

Chargeurs Réunis and Compagnie de Navigation Sud-Atlantique ran their new combo liners to the east coast of South America. Chargeurs Réunis also ran a passenger line from Bordeaux to French West and Equatorial Africa. Transports Maritimes had two of France's largest postwar liners, the *Bretagne* and the *Provence*, on the Mediterranean–South America run. And it seemed that a French armada of its own traded across the western Mediterranean out of Marseilles and Nice. French Line passenger ships went to Corsica and to North Africa. Other firms included Compagnie de Navigation Fraissinet et Cyprien Fabre, Compagnie de Navigation Mixte, and Compagnie de Navigation Paquet.

Eventually the long-distance services were all done in by the inevitable airlines. But while their passengers took to flight, even their profitable cargoes went to bigger, faster, more efficient containerships. The last Messageries Maritimes passenger sailing was the *Pasteur*'s voyage from Buenos Aires and Rio de Janeiro to Le Havre in the summer of 1972. Messageries Maritimes itself was later merged with the CGT to form the CGM, Compagnie Générale Maritime. And as for those North African ships, they have long since been replaced by a new generation of passenger and car-carrying ferries. But there are nostalgic links. One ferry, a 19,000-tonner, is named the *Liberté*. She carries more than 1,600 passengers and 500 cars between Marseilles and North Africa.

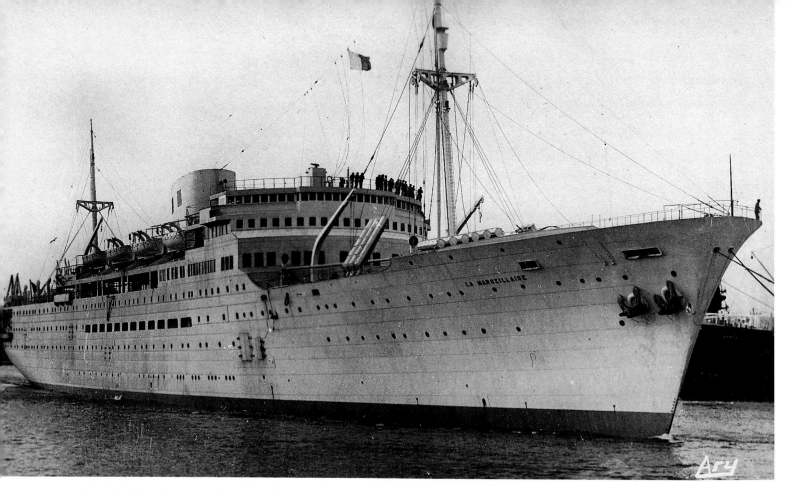

LA MARSEILLAISE

Used on the Marseilles-Saigon service for Messageries Maritimes and therefore represented in North America by the French Line, *La Marseillaise* was the first large passenger liner completed in France after 1939. She came into service in the summer of 1949. Originally laid down in June 1939 (and with completion planned for 1943), her construction went on slowly in the early stages of the war and then, after June 1940, was stopped completely. The Vichy government ordered construction resumed that December, when she was renamed *Maréchal Pétain*, but she was not launched until June 1944. After the war she was renamed *La Marseillaise* and was laid up from 1946 until 1948 while more important freighters were completed in her place. Once in service, she was routed from Marseilles to Port Said, Djibouti (then French Somaliland), Colombo, Singapore,

Saigon, Hong Kong, Manila, Shanghai, and finally Kobe and Yokohama. The round-trip voyage took fifty-three days.

But as France's political status in Southeast Asia changed, ships such as *La Marseillaise* became dispensable. Only eight years old in 1957, she was sold to the Swiss-owned Arosa Line for transatlantic service as their *Arosa Sky*. She later became the *Bianca C.* for Italy's Costa Line before burning and sinking off the Caribbean island of Grenada in October 1961. [Built by Société Provençale de Constructions Navales, La Ciotat, France, 1939–49. 17,321 gross tons; 594 feet long; 75 feet wide. Sulzer diesels, triple screw. Service speed 20 knots. 736 passengers (344 first class, 74 second class, 318 third class).]

Luxury on the run to Saigon! The first-class Veranda Café (*above*) on board *La Marseillaise* was notable for its specially created ceramics on the walls. Boxed plants create the feel of a tropical garden.

In first class the ship had an array of suites and deluxe cabins. The above view shows the sitting room of suite 131. The same space could be used upon request as a private dining room.

CHAMPOLLION

Another Messageries Maritimes liner, the *Champollion*, ran that company's eastern Mediterranean service, from Marseilles and Naples to Alexandria, Port Said, Beirut, and Haifa. Built in 1925, she sailed as an Allied troopship during the war. Originally built with three stacks, she was rebuilt and modernized with a large single funnel in 1950–51. She met with a tragic end, however. While approaching Beirut in heavy seas on December 22, 1952, she stranded. Although she was lying only two hundred yards from the beach, the lifeboats could not be used because of the ferocity of the seas. She later developed a list and then broke in two just aft of the funnel. Just as she was about to capsize on the following day, Beirut rescue crews managed to rescue all but fifteen of those on board. The wreck was later dismantled on the spot. [Built by Société Provençale de Constructions Navales, La Ciotat, France, 1925. 12,546 gross tons; 550 feet long; 62 feet wide. Steam turbines, twin screw. Service speed 17.5 knots. 499 passengers (207 first class, 142 second class, 150 third class).]

LAOS

The last ships to sail the Messageries Maritimes Far Eastern route were three handsome, notably well-decorated combination passenger-cargo liners: the sisters *Cambodge*, *Laos*, and *Viet-Nam*. The *Laos* (shown) completed this trio when she was commissioned in July 1954. They carried passengers in three classes and filled their cargo holds with French manufactured goods for outbound journeys and with the mass produce of Hong Kong and Japan for their return. They ran a monthly schedule from Marseilles to Port Said, Port Suez, Aden, Djibouti, Bombay, Colombo, Singapore, Saigon, Manila, Hong Kong, Kobe, and Yokohama. Their voyages, with first-class fares to Hong Kong set at $450 in the early sixties, were often linked to French Line connections at Le Havre and to some of the transatlantic liners that went to the Mediterranean. Other more elaborate ocean tours were then linked to transpacific liners for the return to the United States, thereby making a complete world voyage of approximately a hundred days.

Later displaced by both the airlines and a new generation of containerships, these three ships were withdrawn by 1969–70. The *Cambodge* became the Greek cruise ship *Stella Solaris*, while the other two became Eastern-owned pilgrim ships. Both later burned and then were scrapped. [Built by Chantiers de la Ciotat, La Ciotat, France, 1954. 13,212 gross tons; 532 feet long; 72 feet wide. Steam turbines, twin screw. Service speed 21 knots. 347 passengers (117 first class, 110 tourist class, 120 third class).]

FERDINAND DE LESSEPS

In its ambitious postwar rebuilding program, Messageries Maritimes built four combination liners for its service to Mauritius. These ships were named the *Ferdinand de Lesseps* (*above*), the *Jean Laborde*, *La Bourdannais*, and the *Pierre Loti*. The *Ferdinand de Lesseps*, launched in July 1951, was the first. One-third of the quartet's five cargo holds were for refrigerated items. The passenger accommodations were divided into three classes: first class consisted of several large suites, other staterooms with private bathroom facilities, several attractive public rooms, a small restaurant (with grand stairwell), and an outdoor swimming pool; tourist class, which was less spacious and comfortable and had more three- and four-berth rooms; and third class, primarily for government troops, police, and workers, who occupied four-berth cabins and small dormitories. The ships were routed from Marseilles to Port Said, Djibouti, Mombasa, Dar-es-Salaam, Majunga, Nossi Bé, Diego Suarez, Tamatave, Réunion, and Mauritius.

Retired in the late sixties, they found prolonged careers mostly under the Greek flag. The *Ferdinand de Lesseps* still sails, for example, as the Mediterranean cruise ship *La Palma*. The former *Jean Laborde* is perhaps best remembered as the *Oceanos*, under which name she made worldwide headlines when she sank off South Africa in August 1991. [Built by Forges et Chantiers de la Gironde, Bordeaux, France, 1951. 10,882 gross tons; 492 feet long; 64 feet wide. B & W type diesels, twin screw. Service speed 17 knots. 240 passengers (88 first class, 112 second class, 40 third class).]

CLAUDE BERNARD

The Paris-based Compagnie Maritime des Chargeurs Réunis ran passenger services on three routes: South America, West Africa, and the Far East. The *Claude Bernard*, introduced in March 1950, was the first of three ships named after French scientists. Based at Le Havre, she sailed from Hamburg; she then called at Antwerp and Le Havre before continuing to Vigo, Leixoes, Madeira, Rio de Janeiro, Santos, Montevideo, and Buenos Aires. Passage fares in the fifties from Le Havre to Buenos Aires ranged from $465 in first class to $240 in third class for the nineteen-day passage.

Teamed with the *Lavoisier* and the *Louis Lumiere*, the *Claude Bernard* had a short career under the French flag. She was sold in 1962 to the East German government, which used her as a training ship out of Rostock. Retired in 1979, she was sold off to Panamanian buyers, who renamed her *Sunrise IV* and then *Pegancia*, before she went to Pakistani ship breakers in 1981. [Built at Ateliers et Chantiers de la Loire, St.-Nazaire, France, 1950. 12,021 gross tons; 537 feet long; 64 feet wide. Sulzer diesels, twin screw. Service speed 17 knots. 324 passengers (94 first class, 230 third class).]

PASTEUR

Although originally intended for the Bordeaux–South America service, the mighty *Pasteur* of Compagnie de Navigation Sud-Atlantique became a troopship soon after completion in 1940 and continued trooping out to Southeast Asia for the French government until late 1956. Early in the following year, she was laid up at Brest. It was suggested that this large, powerful ship be refitted for luxury service with the French Line on its New York run. She could easily replace the aging *Ile de France*. But nothing came to pass, and in the autumn of 1957, she was sold to the North German Lloyd, which moved her to Bremen for a thorough gutting and rebuilding

as its new Atlantic flagship *Bremen*. Coincidentally, when she first arrived at New York in July 1959, she was berthed just across from the *Liberté*. It seems that the two had simply swapped flags—the new German ship was formerly French, while the current French flagship was an ex-German.

The *Bremen* became the Greek cruise ship *Regina Magna* in 1972 and then, in 1977, became an accommodation ship for Middle Eastern workers called the *Saudi Phil I* (and later *Filipinas Saudi I*). On June 6, 1980, while bound for a scrap yard in Taiwan, she keeled over and sank in the Indian Ocean.

VILLE D'ORAN

When built by the French Line in the midthirties, the *Ville d'Oran* (*below*) and her sister ship, the *Ville D'Alger*, were the fastest ships in Mediterranean service. They traded on the North Africa service out of Marseilles, calling at Oran, Algiers, Philippeville, Bône (now Annaba), Mostaganem, and Tunis. Occasionally they were used for short summer cruises. They both survived World War II (although the *Ville d'Alger* had been scuttled by the retreating German forces at Port de Bouc in 1944 and was later salvaged)

and were rebuilt without their original second funnels. Thereafter they traded for the French Line until they were withdrawn in 1965. The *Ville d'Oran* became the *Mount Olympos* for the Typaldos Lines before being broken up in Italy in 1969. [Built by Chantiers et Ateliers de St.-Nazaire, St.-Nazaire, France, 1936. 10,172 gross tons; 484 feet long; 63 feet wide. Steam turbines, twin screw. Service speed 21 knots. 1,154 passengers (149 first class, 334 tourist class, 671 third class).]

SAMPIERO CORSO

Originally built by the French government and managed by Compagnie de Navigation Fraissinet, this ship was scuttled by the Germans during the war and was then salvaged and rebuilt for the French Line. She resumed sailing in 1951. Like several other smaller CGT passenger ships, she worked the Corsica trade from both Marseilles and Nice. Her ports of call included Ajaccio, Bastia, Ile Rousse, and Calvi. She was called to special duty in 1958, when she carried French troops (*below*) across the eastern Mediterranean for the Suez War. [Built by Chantiers et Ateliers de Provence, Port de Bouc, France, 1936. 4,041 gross tons; 345 feet long; 48 feet wide. Steam turbines, twin screw. Service speed 15.5 knots. 824 passengers (113 first class, 115 tourist class, 596 fourth class).]

KAIROUAN

The fastest inter-Mediterranean passenger ship of the early fifties was undoubtedly the *Kairouan*, owned by the Marseilles-based Compagnie de Navigation Mixte. With a service speed of 24 knots, she could make a Marseilles-Algiers passage in seventeen hours. Designed in the late thirties, launched in 1941, scuttled by the Germans in 1944, and salvaged in 1947, she was repaired and completed by 1950. She was the only Mediterranean passenger vessel with turboelectric drive, a feature influenced by the *Normandie*, and the only one using the new Strombos funnel, which had a narrow, tapered design that reduced smoke and soot on deck.

Along with such ships as the French Line's "ville class" of fast passenger ships and other Mixte vessels such as *El Djezair*, *El Mansour*, and the *President de Cazalet*, the *Kairouan* also sailed to Oran and Tunis, sometimes from Port Vendres instead of Marseilles. Her first-class section had air-conditioning, an innovation at that time. Her 133 berths in first class were divided as follows: four de luxe, ten priorité, forty-eight semiluxe, and seventy-one first class. She also had provision for 1,200 tons of general freight or 750 tons of fresh fruit and vegetables. Her three cargo holds could also handle automobiles. [Built by Forges et Chantiers de la Mediterranée, La Seyne, France, 1941–50. 8,589 gross tons; 486 feet long; 60 feet wide. Steam turboelectric, twin screw. Service speed 24 knots. 1,174 passengers (133 first class, 291 tourist class, 750 deck class).]

MERMOZ

When she was completed as the *Jean Mermoz* in May 1957 for the Marseilles–West Africa service of Compagnie de Navigation Fraissinet et Cyprien Fabre, few could have guessed that she would become the last passenger liner under the French flag. Originally designed to carry 854 passengers (144 first class, 140 second class, 110 third class, and 460 troops) as well as cargo, she was withdrawn from that service and rebuilt as a cruise ship at Genoa in 1970. Her new, more streamlined image was reflected in her shortened name, *Mermoz*. Ever since, she has sailed on cruises to ports around the world. While still French-owned, she has been registered in the Bahamas since 1984. With all other French passenger ships long gone, she was the last to fly the tricolor. [Built by Chantiers de l'Atlantique, St.-Nazaire, France, 1957. 13,804 gross tons; 531 feet long; 65 feet wide. B&W-type diesels, twin screw. Service speed 16 knots. 757 passengers, all first class.]

9. END OF THE LINE: THE FRANCE OF 1961

Although it was a moody, rather cold winter afternoon, New York harbor was filled with excitement and anticipation. The date was February 9, 1962, and, unfortunately, it was one of the last of the gala receptions that were once a staple of the port. Escorted by a flotilla of tugs, fireboats, and chartered craft, the brand-new *France* majestically made her way to her berth on the north side of Pier 88. At a very reduced speed she was following in the path of her revered predecessor, the *Normandie*, which had first arrived twenty-two years before. Every horn and whistle and siren saluted the long-awaited $80-million ($400 million in 1996 dollars) flagship, under construction for more than four years.

By the midfifties the French Line was in a major quandary. Both the *Ile de France* and the *Liberté* were growing old. In fact, the *Ile* would be gone within a few years, by 1958. Briefly, a year before, there had been some thought of taking the 1939-built *Pasteur,* then just relieved from Indochinese trooping, and making her over for the North Atlantic as a replacement. Then there were thoughts of a pair of 35,000-tonners. And then, as if to complicate matters even further, there were whispers from across the channel, out of Liverpool, about a possible 75,000-ton superliner replacement for another aging ship, the *Queen Mary*. And what if the Americans finally decided to build the often-suggested sister ship to their speed champion, the *United States?* And, finally, France itself was caught up in the political turmoil of yet another withdrawing colony, Algeria.

The government, especially President de Gaulle, thought a new French superliner might be just the tonic. Like the *Normandie* and others, she would be a morale builder, a centerpiece, a stunning showcase for the decorative and technological brilliance of France. Furthermore, she would be a direct challenge to those two increasingly dowdy British *Queens*. And such a big liner could single-handedly replace both the *Ile de France* and the *Liberté*. And so the steel was ordered and work commenced at St.-Nazaire in September 1957.

Coincidentally, airline traffic equaled that of the Atlantic passenger-liner fleet in 1957; a year later the first jets were flying to London and Paris. By 1959 the airlines had two-thirds of all transatlantic clientele. In hindsight, of course, the folly of building a ship as large and as expensive as the *France* is evident. Even the practical alternative of off-season cruising was only a slight consideration in the overall planning and design. In fact, the CGT proudly boasted that the *France* might be the last major ocean liner to spend most of the year on the Atlantic run. By the early sixties even the mighty *Queen Elizabeth* was known to carry as few as two hundred passengers for a January crossing. But the French persisted.

The *France* actually remained very popular to the end. Her occupancy rarely fell below 90 percent. And she did, in fact, do more cruising than expected. But her economics were such that she was reliant from the start on a government operating subsidy (even when filled to the very last upper berth in tourist class). The end came quite suddenly, after a late summer's crossing from New York in 1974. Her Parisian benefactors had switched their allegiance to the new Concorde. Her ever-increasing injections of francs were gone in a flash. Now only Britain's *QE2* remained.

While the *France* sat at Le Havre, idle and darkened, a parade of potential buyers approached and receded. She might even be scrapped, according to the press. But in the end the Miami-based, Oslo-owned Norwegian Caribbean Lines felt that she had a future—as a tropical cruise ship in the sunny Caribbean. Towed to a West German shipyard, she underwent what was perhaps the most elaborate transformation of any big liner: changing the indoor *France* into the outdoor *Norway*. This last of the great French liners successfully plies those southern waters to this day.

The *France* took four years, three months, and twenty-eight days to create. The French government extended a $14-million loan to the French Line, which itself furnished the remaining $66 million. Initial design studies showed that one 66,000-ton liner would be far superior to two more conventional 30,000-ton ships. They further indicated that a two-class ship was preferable to the more traditional three-class system. Furthermore, with the ship's capacity divided between 500 in first class and 1,500 in tourist class, the tourist section would have full decks from stem to stern, including choice center-ship space formerly allocated exclusively to first class. Her length of 1,035 feet would make her the largest liner ever built: 4 feet longer than Britain's *Queen Elizabeth* and 7 feet longer than her famed predecessor, the *Normandie*.

After her first keel plates were laid on October 7, 1957, huge sections (some weighing as much as 50 tons) came from cities as far away as Orléans, La Ciotat, Le Havre, Lyons, and Lille. Fitting them into place was like arranging the pieces of a huge jigsaw puzzle. [Built by Chantiers de l'Atlantique, St.-Nazaire, France, 1957–61. 66,348 gross tons; 1,035 feet long; 110 feet wide. Steam turbines, quadruple screw. Service speed 30 knots. 1,944 passengers (501 first class, 1,443 tourist class).]

The *France* was given a unique "double bottom" that incorporated an inner keel with storage space for 3,653 tons of fuel, 117 tons of diesel oil, and 682 tons of water. In all, she could carry 8,000 tons of fuel, enough for a full Atlantic round trip without refueling.

Madame Charles de Gaulle was godmother to the *France* at the naming and launch ceremonies on May 11, 1960. The general himself attended and gave an emotional speech on the triumphs of the ship's creation. A day later some two thousand technicians, decorators, artisans, and general contractors invaded the ship to apply the finishing touches, which required another eighteen months.

In the summer of 1960, the rudder and four propeller shafts were installed. It took three weeks to fit the enormous 74-ton rudder and the 53-ton, 60-foot-long shafts, the longest afloat. On board, some 18,000 miles of color-coded wiring was installed, along with 1,300 telephones (1,000 for passengers) and 28 miles of ventilating lines.

The forward funnel, which had been built onshore, was lifted aboard in April 1961. The second soon followed. That summer, the ship was moved to a fitting-out berth at St.-Nazaire.

In November 1961 the *France* had her sea trials. She reached 34.13 knots with only the slightest vibrations. On January 19 she left Le Havre (*above*) on a dress-rehearsal cruise to the Canary Islands—filled to capacity and proving herself admirably.

Just after midday on February 8, 1962, the *France* reached the tip of lower Manhattan (*below*) for her gala maiden reception.

Official welcoming ceremonies, special banquets, press conferences, and tours for travel agents and prospective passengers were all part of the *France*'s extended stay at Pier 88 during her maiden voyage.

On the day of her first departure from New York, four other liners are in view on an ice-filled Hudson River. From left to right are the *Cristoforo Colombo*, Italian Line; the *America* and the *United States*, United States Lines; and then the *Carinthia*, Cunard Line.

The *France*'s unique funnels, which received considerable press attention, were soon compared to sombreros. Radical in design, they were crowned by a pair of ailerons that served as smoke deflectors. The big wing design gave a streamlined look to the funnels themselves while lifting smoke away from the ship and the passenger decks below. In addition, each stack had a special filtering device that removed all solids from the smoke and returned them to the bowels of the ship for disposal into the sea.

Press observers were struck by the *France*'s modern, sometimes severe interiors. There was a splendid array of suites and first-class staterooms along the upper decks (an example is shown above), some large enough to include private dining rooms with special warming kitchens. There was no wood on board, only aluminum, formica, and plastic.

The first-class dining room, the Chambord (*below*), was circular with a domed ceiling and could accommodate four hundred at a single seating. Alongside there was a smaller grill room that Craig Claiborne, a noted culinary authority, called "the greatest French restaurant in the world." Many boarded the *France* for the food alone.

The sun deck kennels had twenty separate quarters, each carpeted and with running water, and the walkways included a New York City fire hydrant and a Paris milestone. The theater could seat 664 passengers on two levels, and there were two swimming pools, one indoor (*above*) and the other on deck covered by a glass shield.

The first-class smoking room (*below*) was considered one of the finest rooms aboard the *France*.

Unlike many other Atlantic liners of the time, the *France* provided advanced amenities even in tourist class. These included a smoking room with dance floor (*above*) and a children's playroom (*below*). Most of the tourist cabins included private showers and toilets. Passage fares in the early 1960s in peak summer season were listed from $470 in first class and from $260 in tourist class. Interested passengers were also furnished with statistics about items carried on each crossing: 246,000 napkins, 21,600 tablecloths, 47,000 pieces of silverware, and 23,700 plates.

The *France* was among the liners in one of the last great gatherings of transatlantic passenger ships at New York. In this view from the summer of 1965, from top to bottom are the *Constitution*, American Export Lines; the *Hanseatic*, Hamburg-Atlantic Line; *United States*, United States Lines; the *Bremen*, North German Lloyd; the *France*; the *Leonardo Da Vinci*, Italian Line; and finally the *Queen Mary* and the *Sylvania*, Cunard Line.

The *France* was often sold out during the summer months and was an amazing 70 percent full at other times. But the glitter slowly began to tarnish by the midsixties as the jets proved furious competition. Winter Atlantic crossings were the first to go. Instead, she was sent more and more to the tropics, carrying 1,349 in a single class. It didn't seem to matter that her pools were indoors and that her open deck spaces were rather limited.

Her reputation drew capacity lists. In this view the *France* is at Port Everglades, Florida (with the *Federico C.* and the laid-up *Queen Elizabeth* in the background). She was then on a sixteen-day cruise that began at New York and called at the Florida port before continuing to St. Thomas, Fort-de-France, Cristobal, Curaçao, and Nassau. Fares for the sixteen-day trip started at $695.

In 1972 the French Line decided to send its celebrated flagship on her first world cruise, a trip that took her around the southern tip of South America (she is too large to pass through the Panama Canal) and then on to such areas as Australia, Hong Kong, India, and South Africa. The planning for such a journey was considerable. A special tanker was dispatched from France, for example, for a refueling rendezvous off Rio de Janeiro. Giant consignments of extra linens and special supplies were flown ahead. There was a continual airlift to and from Paris for weary crew members. As for special passenger needs, one prosperous guest had his favorite brand of champagne flown to Hong Kong to meet the ship.

Two years later, the *France* was at its worst—the Atlantic trade had declined sharply while the American cruise trades had grown more and more competitive. To complicate matters, the price of a barrel of fuel oil had suddenly jumped from $35 to $95. The French government would have had to increase its annual subsidy from $14 million to $24 million. Instead, the Paris ministers voted to support the new Concorde fleet for Air France. The French Line had no choice but to withdraw the liner. In September 1974 crew members mutinied in the channel, just off Le Havre, demanding that she be restored and asking for 35 percent wage increases. The attempt quickly failed, and the *France* was sent to an old pier in the backwaters of Le Havre.

On a winter afternoon, the *Mary* is outbound on a deserted Hudson.
She is seen from the cliffs of Weehawken, New Jersey.

A small maintenance crew looked after the world's longest liner. Her public rooms were dark and lifeless, the furniture protected by dust covers.

The library—writing room (*above*) and the enclosed children's promenade (*below*) are shown.

In 1976 an Arab millionaire, Akram Ojjeh, bought the liner from the French government for $22 million. His plan was to fill her with antique French furniture (at an additional cost of $15 million) and turn her into a combination floating museum of French culture and history and hotel-casino moored off Daytona Beach, Florida. The plan was stillborn, and the ship, amassing hefty dockage fees, went back on the sales lists. There were rumors that the Soviets wanted her as a hotel ship berthed along the Black Sea; the Chinese as a floating industrial trade fair; and, worse still, that Far Eastern scrap merchants were eager to lay hold of her. Instead, in 1979 the *France* passed into the hands of the Oslo-headquartered, Miami-based Norwegian Caribbean Lines, then one of the most successful firms in the lucrative Caribbean cruise business. The transfer cost $18 million, and that August (as shown) the ship was towed to the Hapag-Lloyd shipyards at Bremerhaven, West Germany, to undergo an $80-million rejuvenation and transformation into a tropical cruise ship. The indoor *France* became the outdoor *Norway*.

The *Norway* hoisted the Norwegian colors along with those (by special decree) of the United Nations as a salute to the more than twenty-five nationalities represented in her crew. The keys to the liner's operations were efficiency and economy. Using only one engine room would create a fuel-saving service speed of 16 knots. The staff was reduced from the French level of 1,110 to 800; the capacity was increased from 2,044 to 2,181. On board some original fittings remained while others were replaced with outdoor pools, lido decks, shopping arcades, discos, soda fountains, and slot machines.

In May 1980 the *Norway* crossed on a special Atlantic voyage from Oslo to New York via Southampton (she is shown arriving off lower Manhattan) and then took up her position in the Miami-Caribbean trade. By 1995 she was the last survivor of the French Line fleet.

BIBLIOGRAPHY

Bonsor, N. R. P. *North Atlantic Seaway*. Prescot, Lancashire: T. Stephenson & Sons Limited, 1955.

Braynard, Frank O. *Lives of the Liners*. New York: Cornell Maritime Press, 1947.

Braynard, Frank O., and William H. Miller. *Fifty Famous Liners*. Vols. 1–3. Cambridge, England: Patrick Stephens Limited, 1982–87.

Coleman, Terry. *The Liners*. New York: G. P. Putnam's Sons, 1977.

Crowdy, Michael, ed. *Marine News*. Kendal, Cumbria: World Ship Society, 1965–95.

Devol, George, ed. *Ocean and Cruise News*. Stamford, Connecticut: World Ocean & Cruise Society, 1980–95.

Dunn, Laurence. *Passenger Liners*. Southampton, England: Adlard Coles Limited, 1961.

———. *Passenger Liners*. Rev. ed. Southampton, England: Adlard Coles Limited, 1965.

Eisele, Peter, and William Rau, eds. *Steamboat Bill*. New York: Steamship Historical Society of America Inc., 1966–95.

Horton White, A. G. *Ships of the North Atlantic*. London: Sampson Low, Marston and Company Limited, 1937.

Kludas, Arnold. *Great Passenger Ships of the World*. Vols. 1–5. Cambridge, England: Patrick Stephens Limited, 1972–76.

———. *Great Passenger Ships of the World*. Vol. 6. Cambridge, England: Patrick Stephens Limited, 1986.

———. *Great Passenger Ships of the World Today*. Sparkford, England: Patrick Stephens Limited, 1992.

Maxtone-Graham, *The Only Way to Cross*. New York: The Macmillan Company, 1972.

Miller, William H. *The Last Atlantic Liners*. London: Conway Maritime Press Limited, 1985.

———. *The Last Blue Water Liners*. London: Conway Maritime Press Limited, 1986.

Official Steamship Guide. New York: Transportation Guides Inc., 1937–63.

Ships and Sailing. Milwaukee, Wisconsin: Kalmbach Publishing Company, 1950–60.

Smith, Eugene W. *Passenger Ships of the World Past and Present*. Boston: George H. Dean Company, 1963.

Towline. New York: Moran Towing and Transportation Company, 1950–95.

Via Port. New York: Port Authority of New York and New Jersey, 1955–95.

INDEX OF SHIPS ILLUSTRATED